fun Start
KOREAN
WORKBOOK FOR KIDS 1

This book belongs to

STELLARSOL®
CREATIVE LEARNING

Korean
Pronunciation vs. Romanization

We used official romanization per the National Institute of Korean Language, but English letters may not precisely match Korean sounds. Romanization aids beginners in phonetic pronunciation while learning Hangul. Practice accurate pronunciation by listening to native speakers.

FREE downloadable audio files are available on
stellarsol.net/resources

Thank You
Your Support is Invaluable

You're the essence of our business. We hope you love your workbook as much as we enjoyed creating it!

love your book? let us know!

★ ★ ★ ★ ★

Please be so kind as to leave a review for us.

Table of Contents

How the Korean Alphabet, Hangul Works

Syllable **Without** a Final Consonant (a.k.a. 받침 [bat-chim])

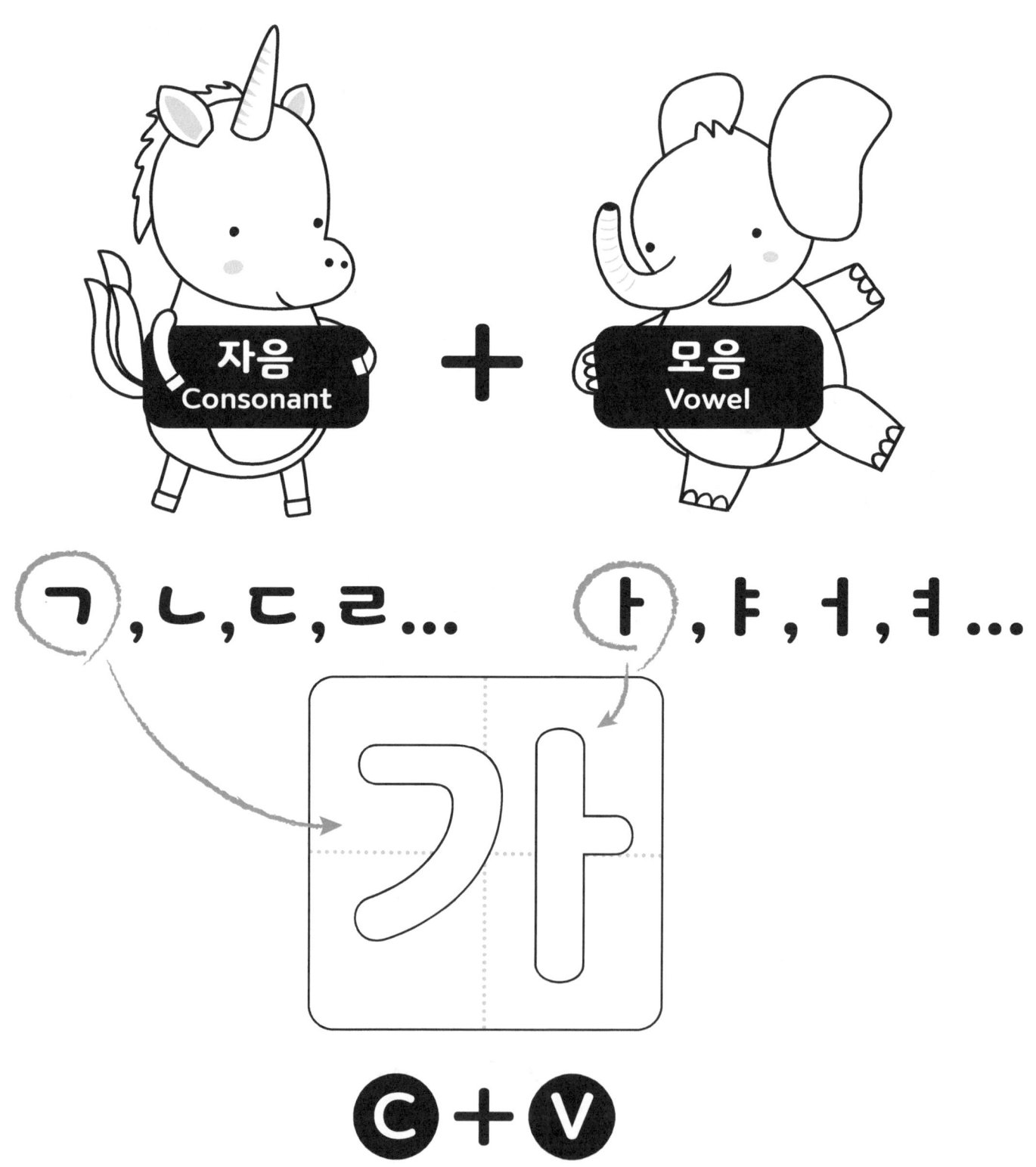

C + V

Syllable **With** a Final Consonant (a.k.a. 받침 [bat-chim])

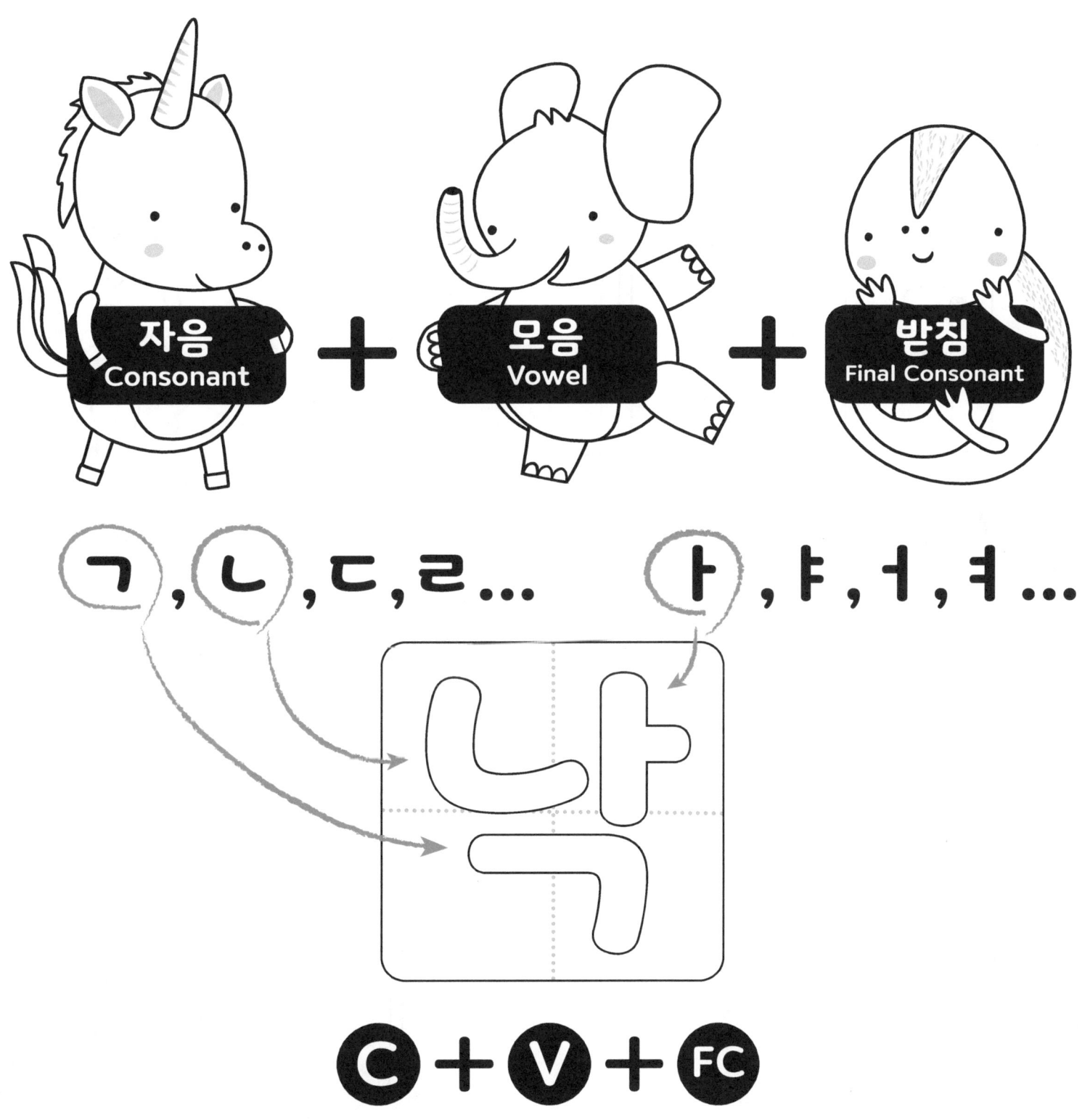

What are 10 Basic Vowels?

아 [a]

악어 [ak-eo] Alligator

야 [ya]

양 [yang] Sheep

어 [eo]

얼룩말 [eol-ruk-mal] Zebra

여 [yeo]

여우 [yeo-u] Fox

오 [o]

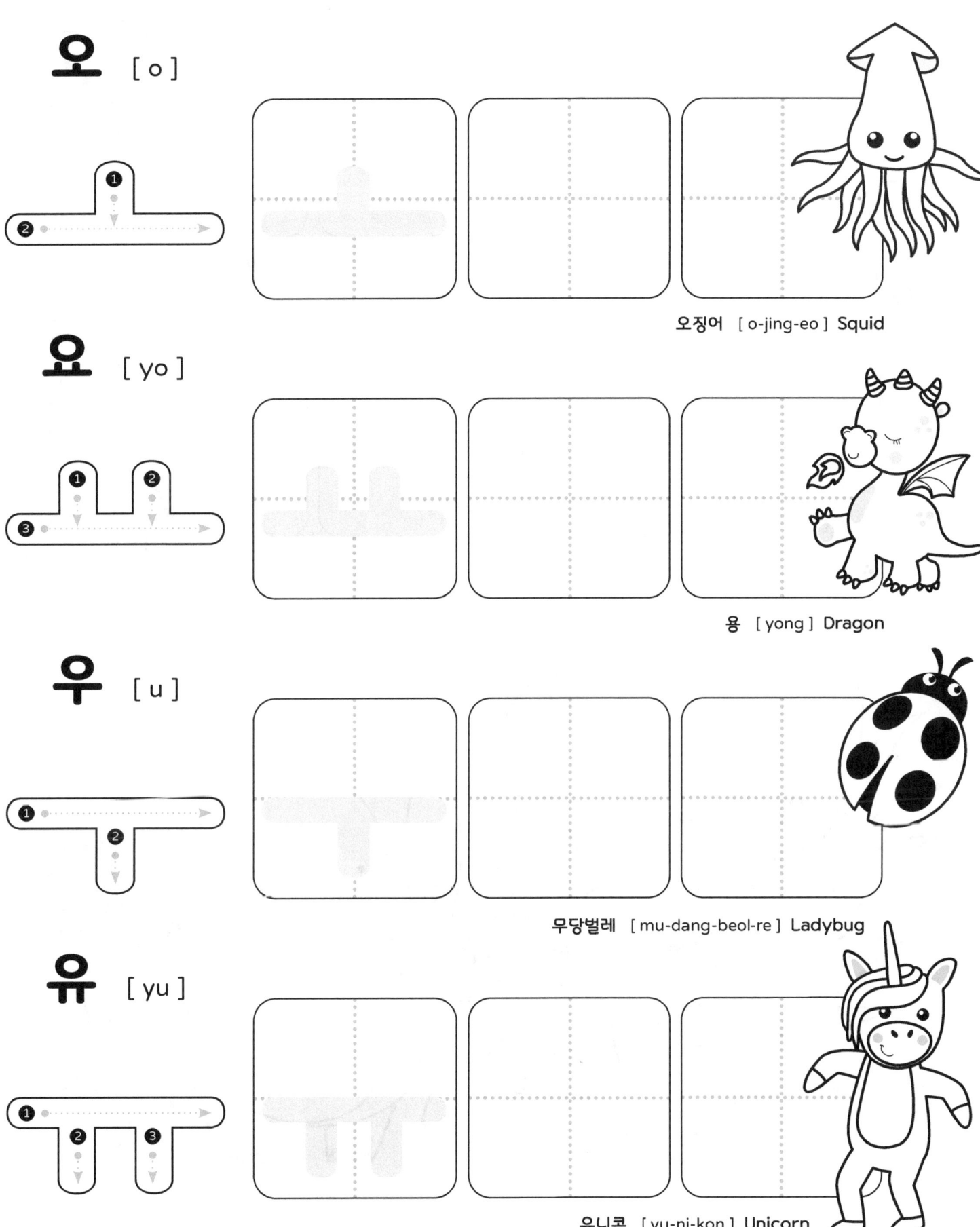

오징어 [o-jing-eo] Squid

요 [yo]

용 [yong] Dragon

우 [u]

무당벌레 [mu-dang-beol-re] Ladybug

유 [yu]

유니콘 [yu-ni-kon] Unicorn

으 [eu]

①

늘보원숭이 [neul-bo-won-sung-i] Loris

이 [i]

①

기린 [gi-rin] Giraffe

14 Basic Consonants

기역 [gi-yeok]

ROMANIZATION

[g/k]

강아지 [gang-a-ji] Puppy

Color

가방

[ga-bang]

Bag

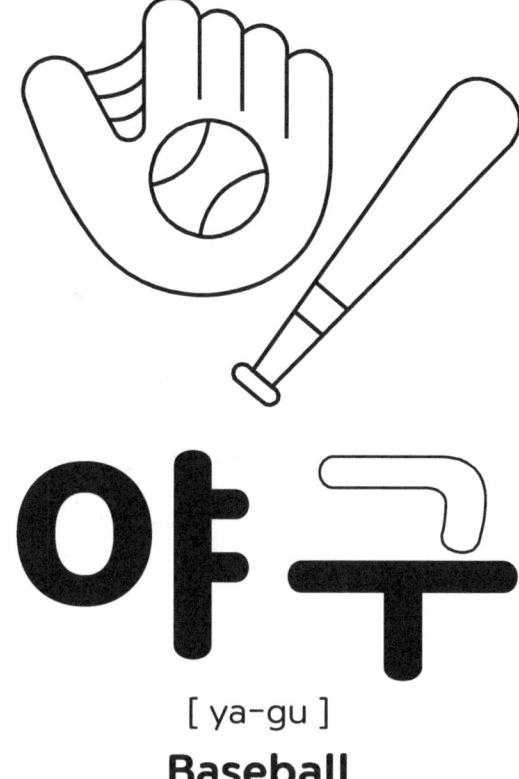

야구

[ya-gu]

Baseball

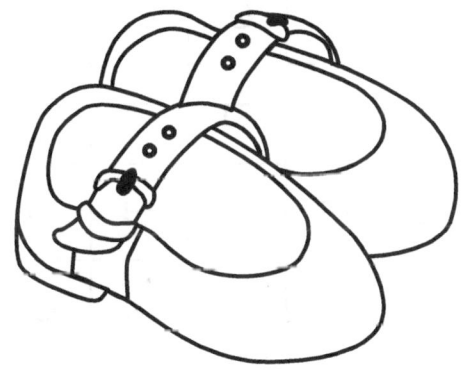

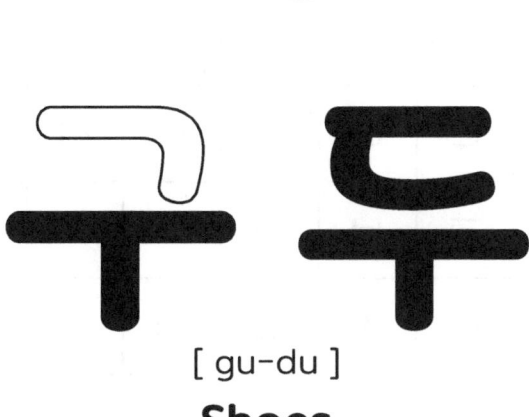

구두

[gu-du]

Shoes

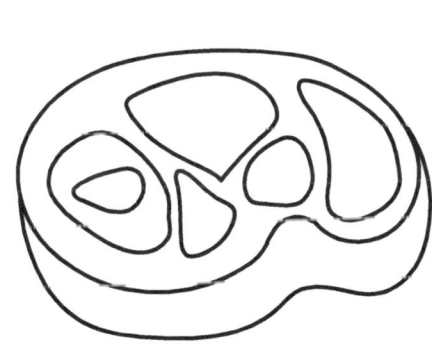

고기

[go-gi]

Meat

Find and Color

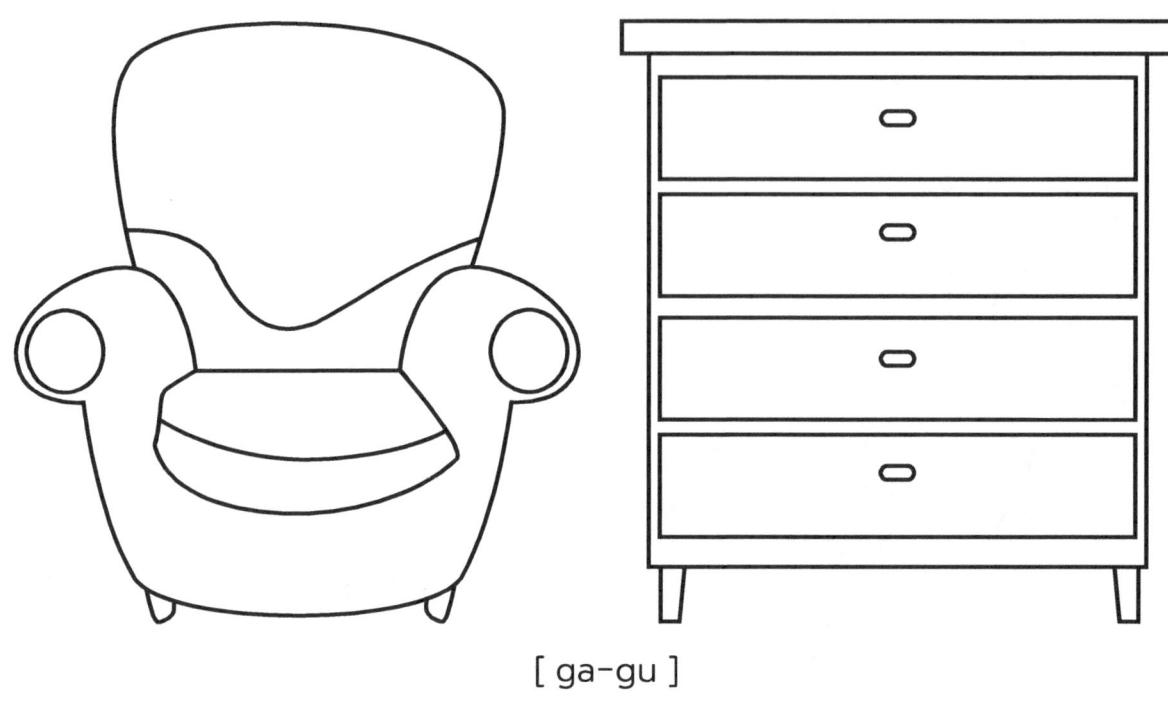

[ga-gu]
Furniture

ㄹ	ㅂ	ㄴ	ㅂ	ㄴ	ㅅ	ㅎ	ㅂ	ㄴ	ㄷ	ㄴ	ㅂ	ㅍ	ㅇ
ㅊ	ㄱ	ㄱ	ㄱ	ㄹ	ㄱ	ㅊ	ㅅ	ㄱ	ㄱ	ㄱ	ㄱ	ㄱ	ㅇ
ㅂ	ㅇ	ㅅ	ㄱ	ㄹ	ㄱ	ㅅ	ㅊ	ㄹ	ㄹ	ㅍ	ㅂ	ㄱ	ㅂ
ㅊ	ㅂ	ㅊ	ㄱ	ㅅ	ㄱ	ㄱ	ㅍ	ㄷ	ㅇ	ㅇ	ㅅ	ㄴ	ㅍ
ㅅ	ㄴ	ㅂ	ㄱ	ㅊ	ㄱ	ㅊ	ㅊ	ㄱ	ㄱ	ㄱ	ㄱ	ㄱ	ㅎ
ㄷ	ㅇ	ㅇ	ㄱ	ㄷ	ㄱ	ㅇ	ㄷ	ㄹ	ㄷ	ㄱ	ㄴ	ㅂ	ㄴ
ㅂ	ㅂ	ㅊ	ㄹ	ㄹ	ㄹ	ㅅ	ㅊ	ㄹ	ㅂ	ㄱ	ㅅ	ㅅ	ㅍ
ㅎ	ㄷ	ㅇ	ㅇ	ㅊ	ㅅ	ㅇ	ㄷ	ㄹ	ㅅ	ㅍ	ㅂ	ㅍ	ㅎ

Let's Make a Sound!

Color the consonant and trace the letters.

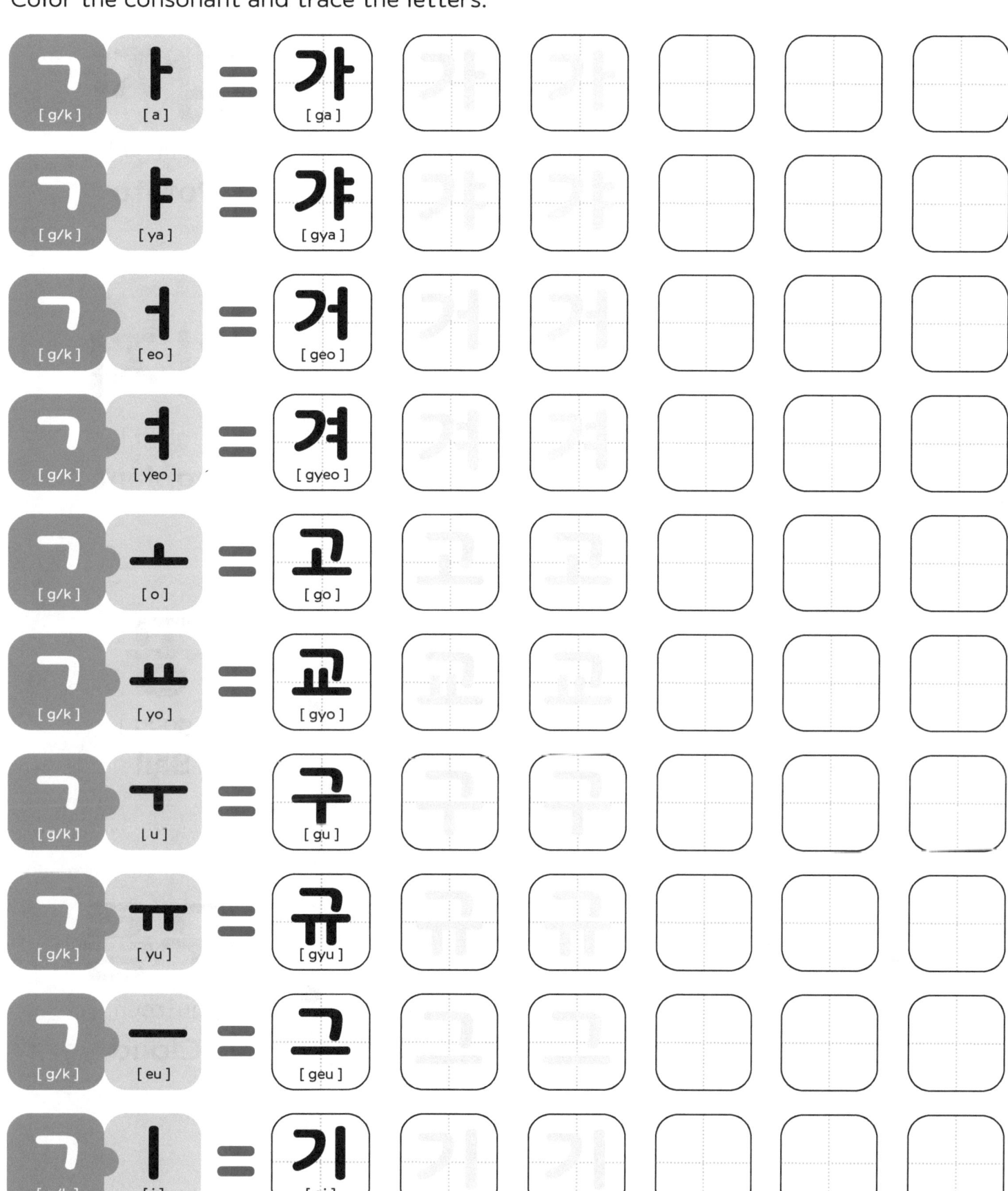

ㄱ [g/k] ㅏ [a] = 가 [ga]

ㄱ [g/k] ㅑ [ya] = 갸 [gya]

ㄱ [g/k] ㅓ [eo] = 거 [geo]

ㄱ [g/k] ㅕ [yeo] = 겨 [gyeo]

ㄱ [g/k] ㅗ [o] = 고 [go]

ㄱ [g/k] ㅛ [yo] = 교 [gyo]

ㄱ [g/k] ㅜ [u] = 구 [gu]

ㄱ [g/k] ㅠ [yu] = 규 [gyu]

ㄱ [g/k] ─ [eu] = 그 [geu]

ㄱ [g/k] ㅣ [i] = 기 [gi]

Match Words with Pictures

감자
[gam-ja]
Potato

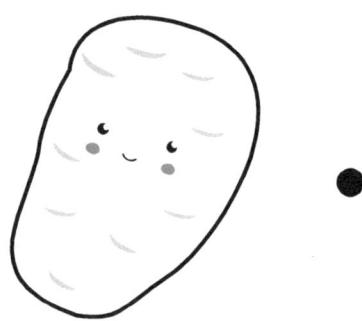

가지
[ga-ji]
Eggplant

공
[gong]
Ball

구름
[gu-reum]
Cloud

Color By the Letters

고양이

[go-yang-i]
Cat

가: 검정색 (Black)　**거:** 노란색 (Yellow)　**고:** 빨간색 (Red)
구: 파란색 (Blue)　**그:** 회색 (Gray)　**기:** 분홍색 (Pink)

Cut & Paste

Cut and paste the matching words and write it below. Find letter pieces from page 125.

기차

[gi-cha]
Train

거미

[geo-mi]
Spider

기도

[gi-do]
Pray

고추

[go-chu]
Pepper

구슬

[gu-seul]
Marble

기타

[gi-ta]
Guitar

Vocabulary Builder

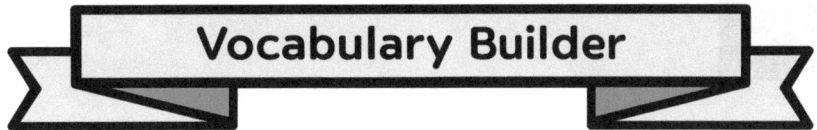

가족 | *family*

Cut and paste the matching words. Find letter pieces from page 125.

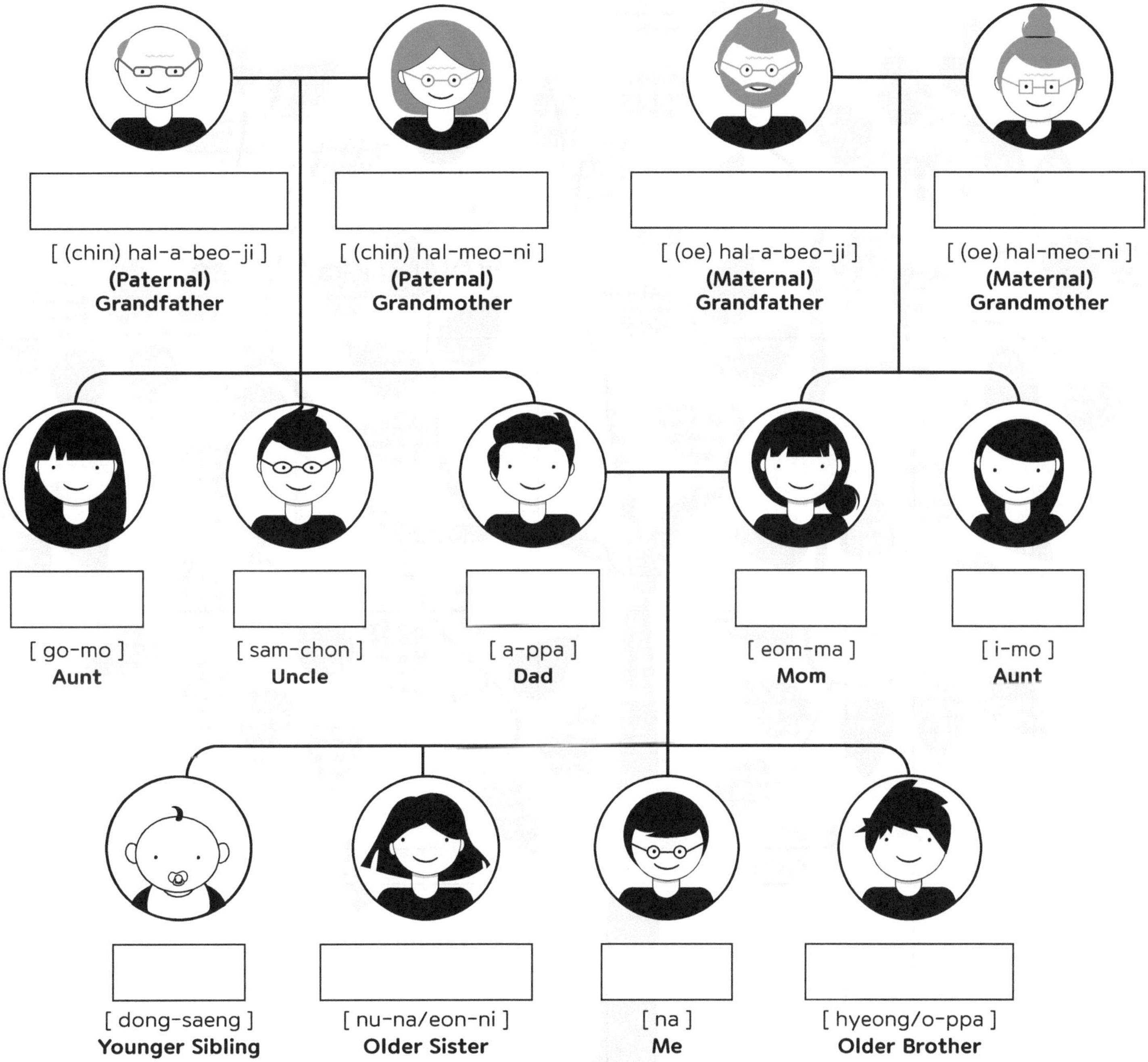

[(chin) hal-a-beo-ji]
(Paternal) Grandfather
[(chin) hal-meo-ni]
(Paternal) Grandmother
[(oe) hal-a-beo-ji]
(Maternal) Grandfather
[(oe) hal-meo-ni]
(Maternal) Grandmother
[go-mo]
Aunt
[sam-chon]
Uncle
[a-ppa]
Dad
[eom-ma]
Mom
[i-mo]
Aunt
[dong-saeng]
Younger Sibling
[nu-na/eon-ni]
Older Sister
[na]
Me
[hyeong/o-ppa]
Older Brother

니은 [ni-eun]

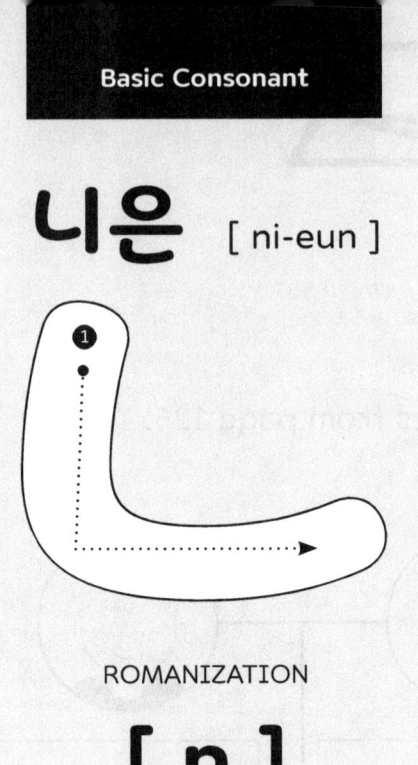

ROMANIZATION

[n]

낙타 [nak-ta] **Camel**

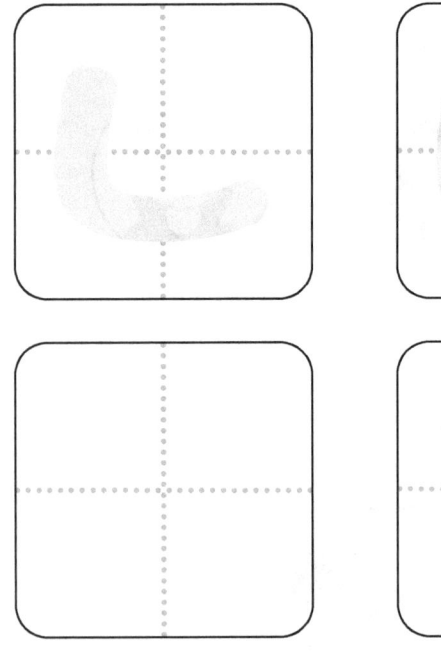
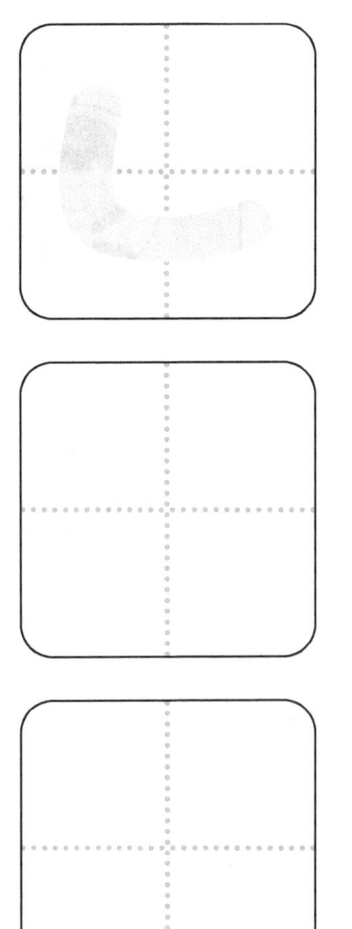
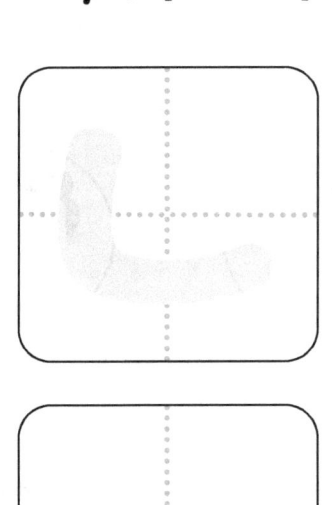
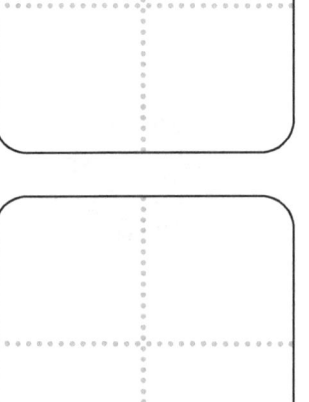
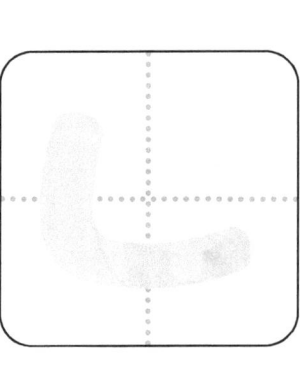
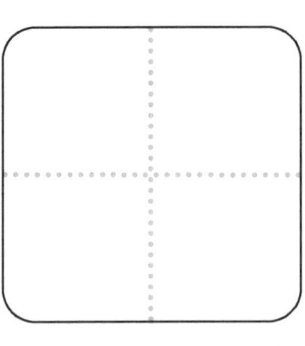
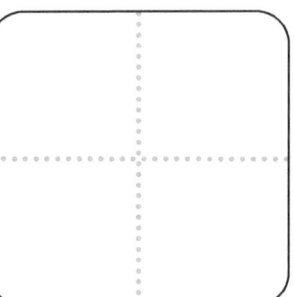

Color

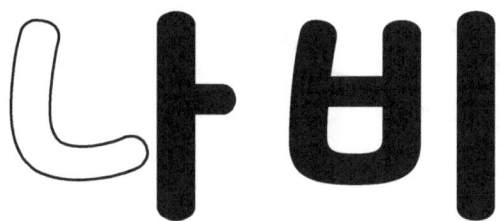

[na-bi]

Butterfly

누나

[nu-na]

Older Sister*

*A younger male to call an older female or sibling

[nam-ja]

Man/Male

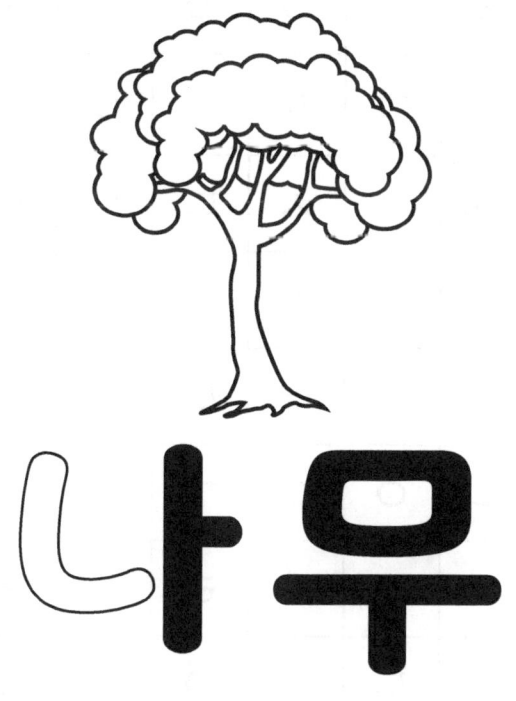

나무

[na-mu]

Tree

Find and Color ㄴ

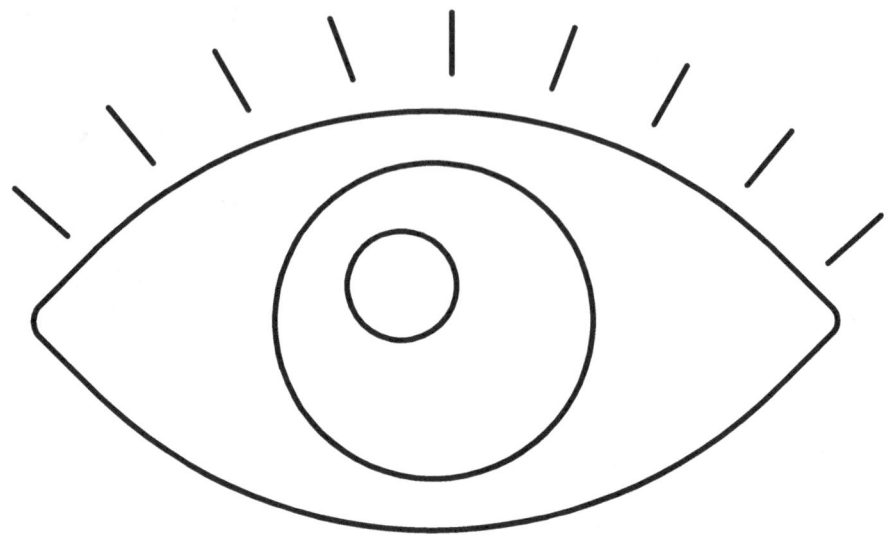

[nun]

Eye

ㄹ	ㅂ	ㅁ	ㅂ	ㄴ	ㅅ	ㅎ	ㅂ	ㅍ	ㄷ	ㅈ	ㅂ	ㅍ	ㅇ
ㅊ	ㄱ	ㅍ	ㄱ	ㄴ	ㄱ	ㅊ	ㅅ	ㄱ	ㅈ	ㄷ	ㅍ	ㅋ	ㅇ
ㅂ	ㅇ	ㅅ	ㄷ	ㄴ	ㄴ	ㄴ	ㄴ	ㄴ	ㄴ	ㄴ	ㄴ	ㅂ	ㄱ	ㅂ
ㅊ	ㅂ	ㅊ	ㄱ	ㅅ	ㄱ	ㄱ	ㅍ	ㄷ	ㅇ	ㅇ	ㅅ	ㄷ	ㅍ
ㅅ	ㅌ	ㅂ	ㄴ	ㄴ	ㄴ	ㄴ	ㄴ	ㄴ	ㄴ	ㄴ	ㄴ	ㄱ	ㅎ
ㄷ	ㅇ	ㅇ	ㄱ	ㄷ	ㄱ	ㅇ	ㄴ	ㄹ	ㄷ	ㄱ	ㅁ	ㅂ	ㄷ
ㅂ	ㅂ	ㅊ	ㄹ	ㄴ	ㄹ	ㅅ	ㅊ	ㄹ	ㅂ	ㄱ	ㅅ	ㅅ	ㅍ
ㅎ	ㄷ	ㅇ	ㅇ	ㄴ	ㄴ	ㄴ	ㄴ	ㄴ	ㄴ	ㄴ	ㄴ	ㅂ	ㅍ	ㅎ

Let's Make a Sound!

Color the consonant and trace the letters.

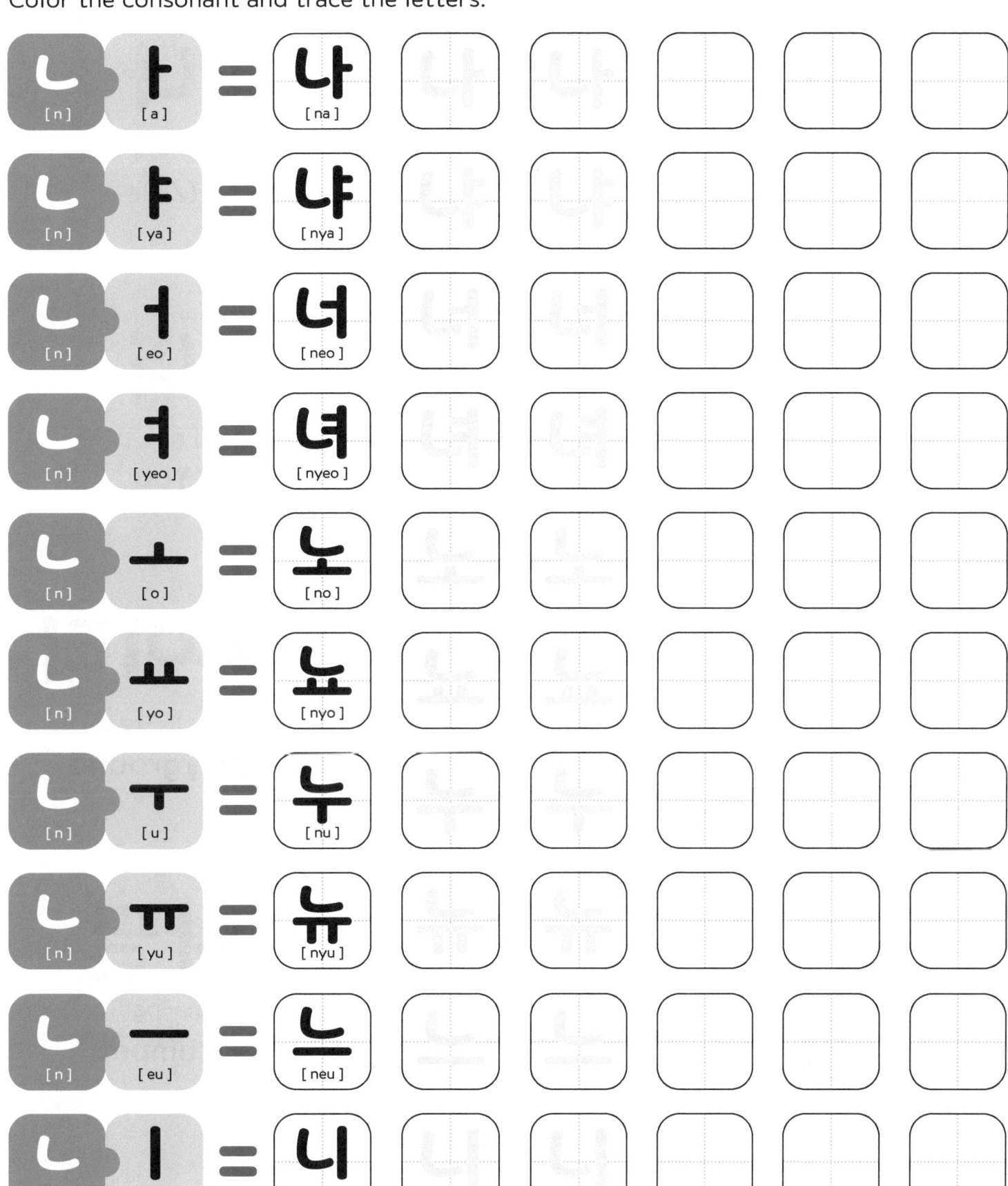

ㄴ [n] + ㅏ [a] = 나 [na]

ㄴ [n] + ㅑ [ya] = 냐 [nya]

ㄴ [n] + ㅓ [eo] = 너 [neo]

ㄴ [n] + ㅕ [yeo] = 녀 [nyeo]

ㄴ [n] + ㅗ [o] = 노 [no]

ㄴ [n] + ㅛ [yo] = 뇨 [nyo]

ㄴ [n] + ㅜ [u] = 누 [nu]

ㄴ [n] + ㅠ [yu] = 뉴 [nyu]

ㄴ [n] + ㅡ [eu] = 느 [neu]

ㄴ [n] + ㅣ [i] = 니 [ni]

Match Words with Pictures

나
[na]
I/Me

너
[neo]
You

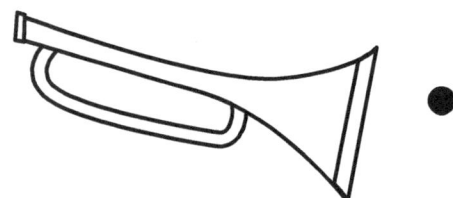

놀이터
[nol-i-teo]
Playground

나팔
[na-pal]
Trumpet

Color By the Letters

너구리

[neo-gu-ri]

Raccoon

나: 검정색 (Black) **너:** 노란색 (Yellow) **노:** 빨간색 (Red)

누: 파란색 (Blue) **느:** 회색 (Gray) **니:** 살구색 (Apricot)

Cut & Paste

Cut and paste the matching words and write it below. Find letter pieces from page 125.

[nun]
Snow

[na-ra]
Country

[nin-ja]
Ninja

[nyu-yok]
New York

[na-sa]
Screw

[nong-bu]
Farmer

Vocabulary Builder

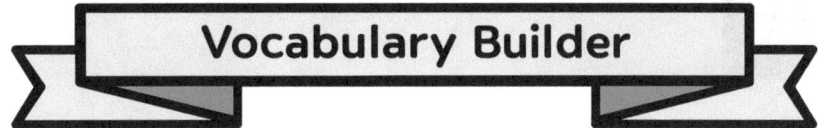

신체 부위 | Parts of the Body

Cut and paste the matching words. Find letter pieces from page 125.

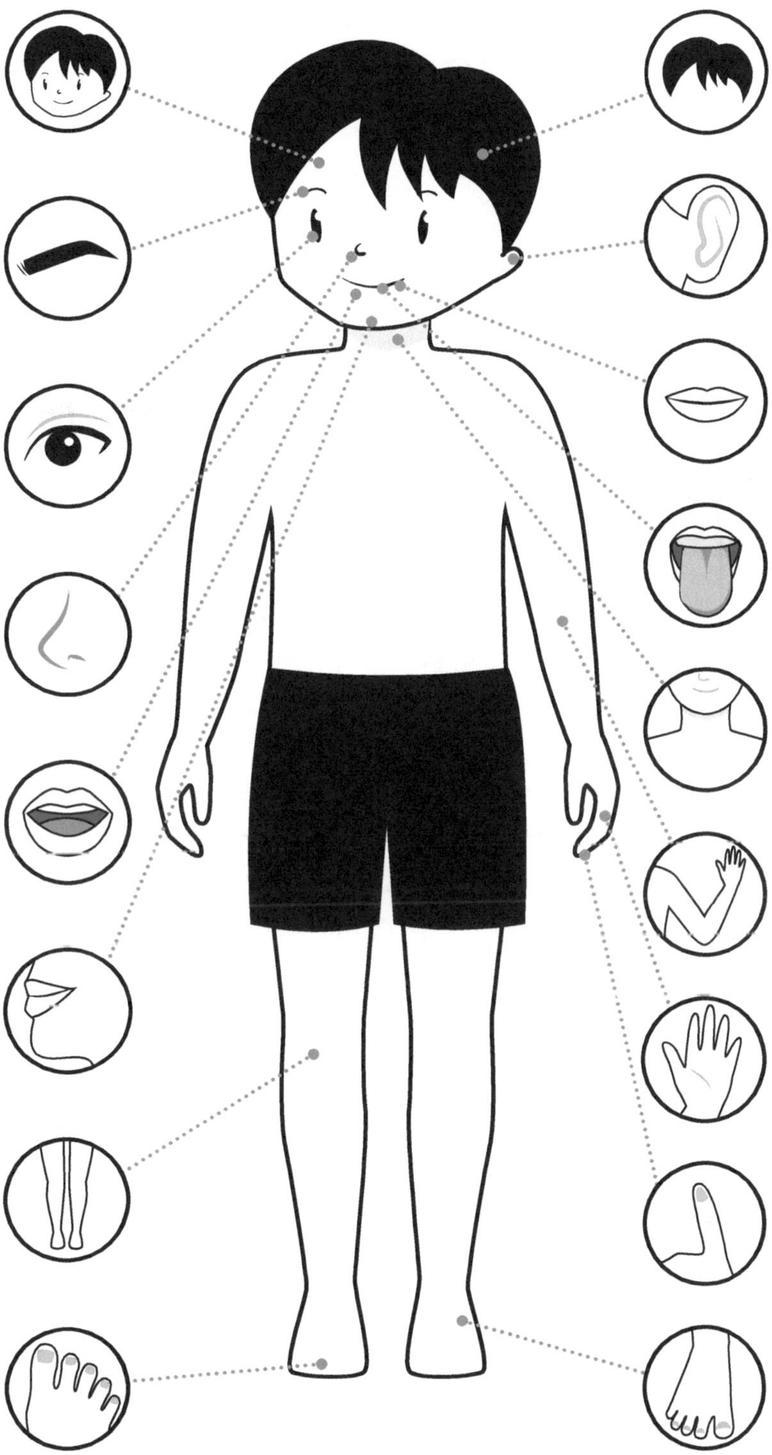

[eol-gul]
Face

[nun-sseop]
Eyebrow

[nun]
Eye

[ko]
Nose

[ip]
Mouth

[teok]
Chin

[da-ri]
Leg

[bal-ga-rak]
Toe

[meo-ri-ka-rak]
Hair

[gwi]
Ear

[ip-sul]
Lips

[hyeo]
Tongue

[mok]
Neck

[pal]
Arm

[son]
Hand

[son-ga-rak]
Finger

[bal]
Foot

디귿 [di-geut]

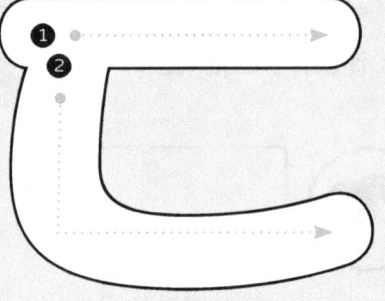

ROMANIZATION

[d]

달 [dal] **Moon**

Color ㄷ

다리
[da-ri]
Legs or Bridge

당근
[dang-geun]
Carrot

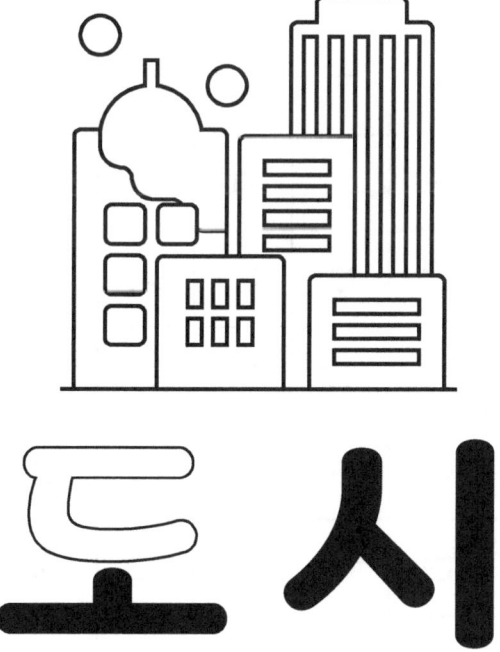

도시
[do-si]
City

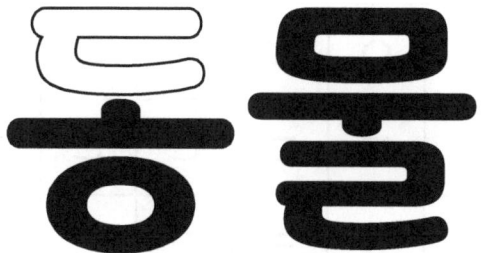

동물
[dong-mul]
Animals

Find and Color

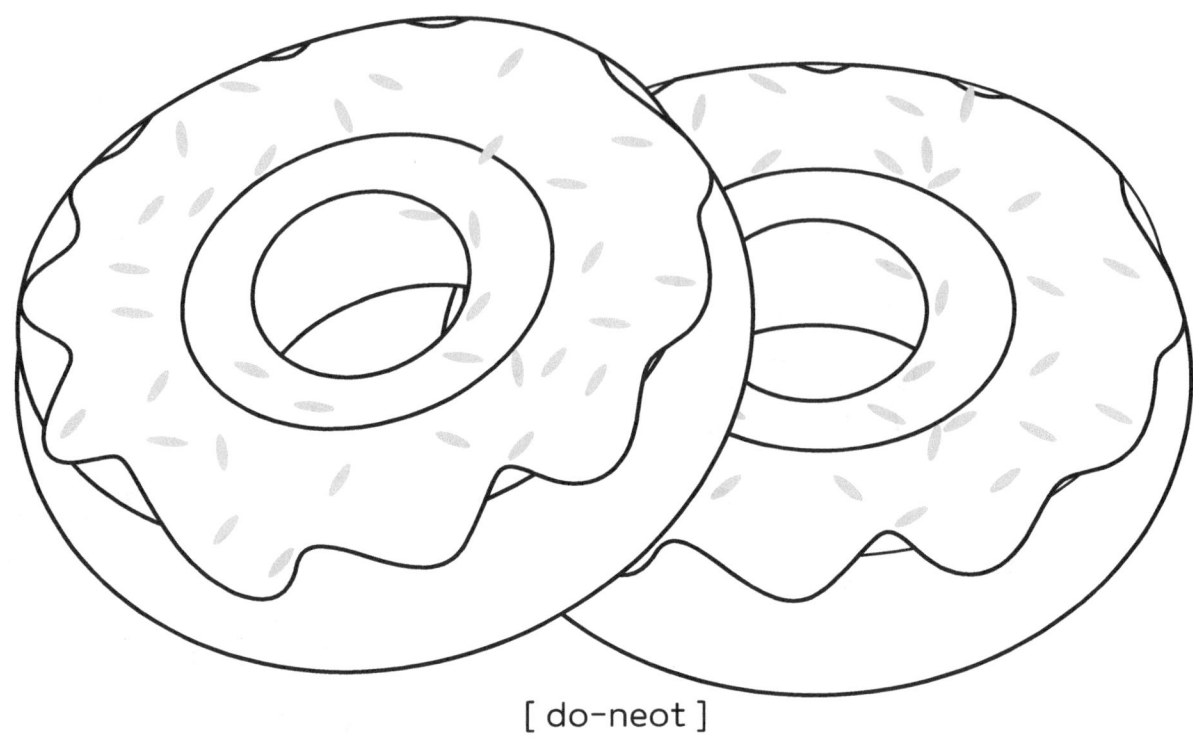

[do-neot]

Donut

ㄷ	ㄷ	ㄷ	ㄷ	ㄷ	ㅅ	ㅎ	ㄷ	ㄴ	ㅇ	ㄴ	ㅂ	ㄷ	ㅇ
ㄷ	ㄱ	ㅊ	ㄱ	ㅋ	ㄱ	ㅊ	ㄷ	ㅅ	ㄱ	ㄷ	ㄷ	ㄷ	ㅋ
ㄷ	ㅇ	ㅅ	ㅊ	ㄹ	ㅌ	ㅅ	ㄷ	ㄹ	ㅅ	ㅍ	ㅂ	ㄷ	ㅂ
ㄷ	ㄷ	ㄷ	ㄷ	ㄷ	ㅍ	ㄱ	ㄷ	ㄷ	ㄷ	ㄷ	ㅅ	ㄷ	ㅍ
ㄱ	ㅊ	ㄱ	ㅋ	ㄱ	ㅊ	ㅋ	ㅊ	ㄱ	ㅎ	ㅋ	ㅌ	ㅅ	ㅎ
ㅈ	ㅇ	ㄷ	ㄱ	ㅌ	ㄴ	ㅇ	ㅈ	ㄹ	ㅅ	ㄷ	ㄴ	ㅂ	ㄴ
ㄷ	ㄷ	ㄷ	ㄷ	ㄷ	ㅈ	ㅅ	ㅋ	ㄹ	ㄷ	ㄱ	ㄷ	ㅅ	ㅍ
ㅈ	ㅅ	ㅋ	ㄹ	ㅊ	ㅅ	ㅇ	ㅌ	ㄷ	ㅅ	ㅍ	ㅂ	ㄷ	ㅎ

Let's Make a Sound!

Color the consonant and trace the letters.

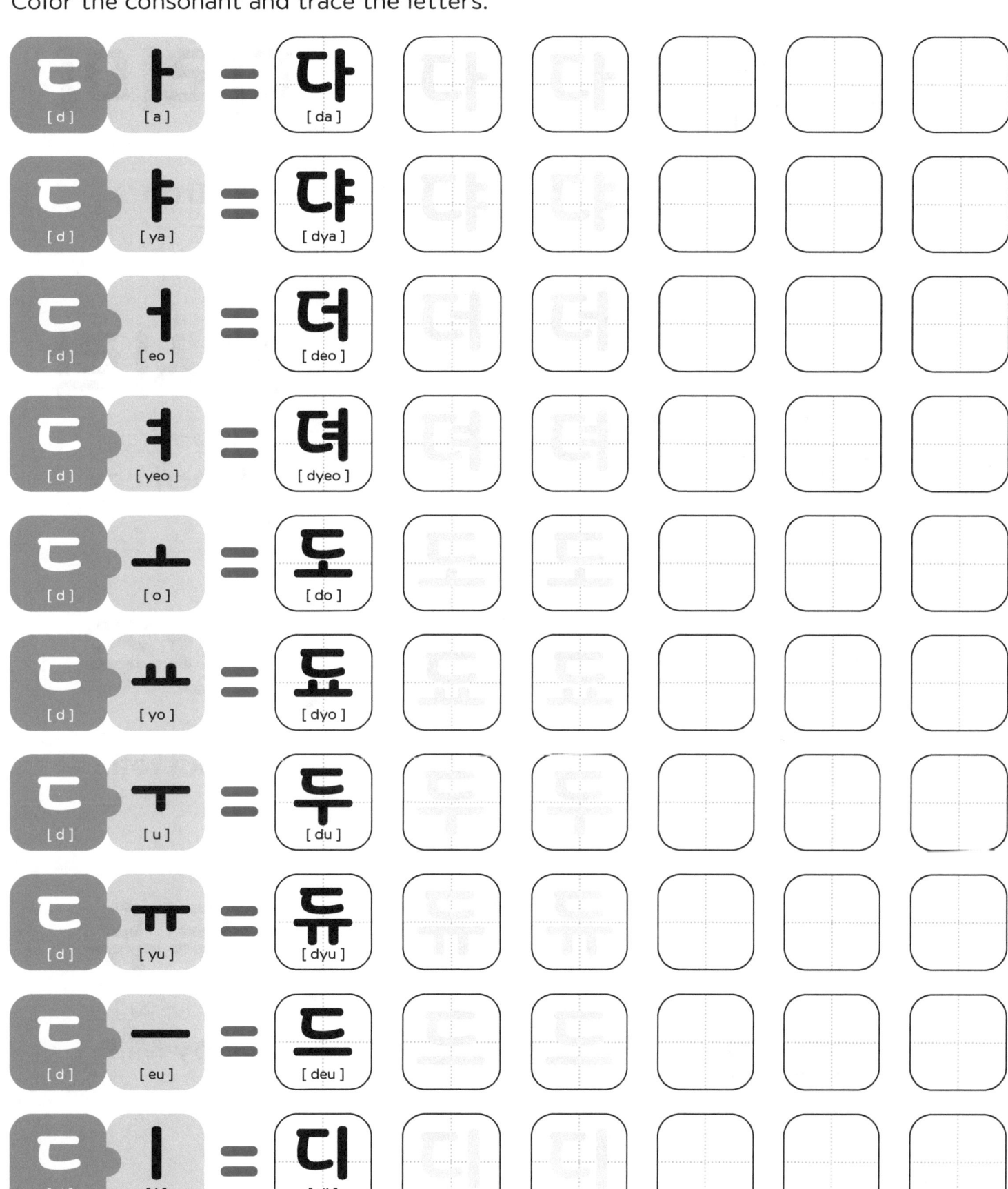

ㄷ [d]	ㅏ [a]	=	다 [da]	다	다			
ㄷ [d]	ㅑ [ya]	=	댜 [dya]	댜	댜			
ㄷ [d]	ㅓ [eo]	=	더 [deo]	더	더			
ㄷ [d]	ㅕ [yeo]	=	뎌 [dyeo]	뎌	뎌			
ㄷ [d]	ㅗ [o]	=	도 [do]	도	도			
ㄷ [d]	ㅛ [yo]	=	됴 [dyo]	됴	됴			
ㄷ [d]	ㅜ [u]	=	두 [du]	두	두			
ㄷ [d]	ㅠ [yu]	=	듀 [dyu]	듀	듀			
ㄷ [d]	ㅡ [eu]	=	드 [deu]	드	드			
ㄷ [d]	ㅣ [i]	=	디 [di]	디	디			

Match Words with Pictures

다리미
[da-ri-mi]
Iron

도시락
[do-si-rak]
Lunch box

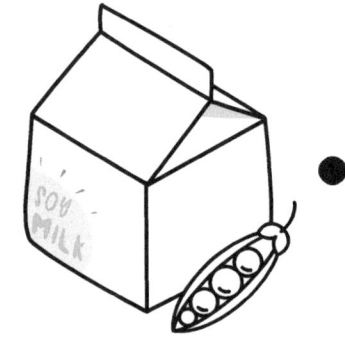

단추
[dan-chu]
Button

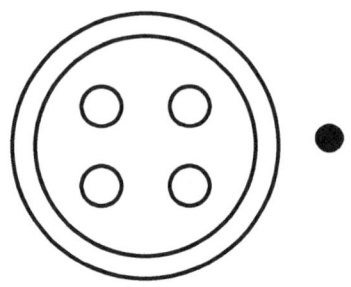

두유
[du-yu]
Soy Milk

Color By the Letters

도리
[do-ri]
Dory

다: 검정색 (Black) **더:** 하늘색 (Light Blue) **도:** 빨간색 (Red) **됴:** 보라색 (Purple)

두: 초록색 (Green) **듀:** 노란색 (Yellow) **드:** 파란색 (Blue) **디:** 분홍색 (Pink)

Cut & Paste

Cut and paste the matching words and write it below. Find letter pieces from page 127.

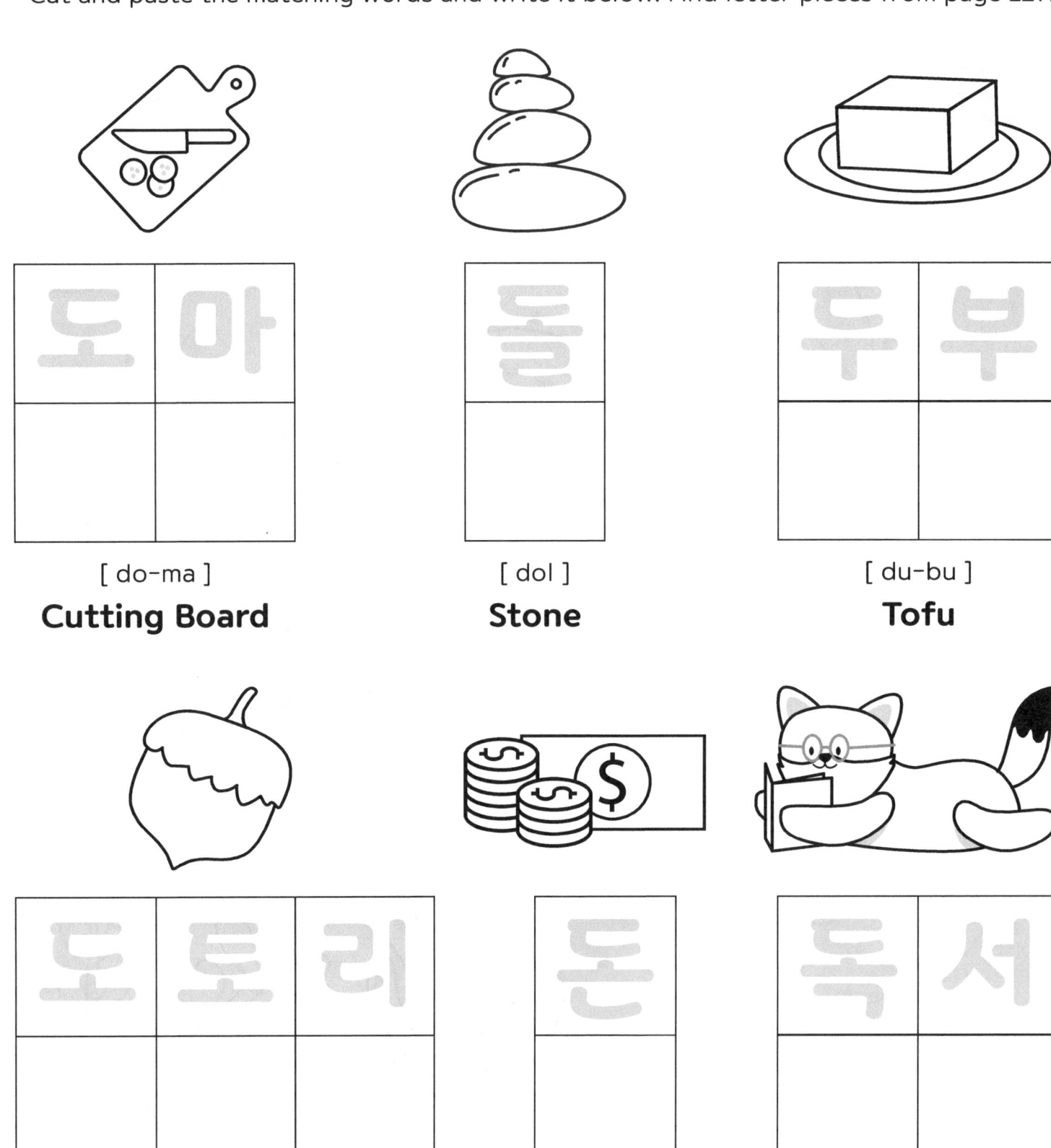

[do-ma]
Cutting Board

[dol]
Stone

[du-bu]
Tofu

[do-to-ri]
Acorn

[don]
Money

[dok-seo]
Reading

계절 | Seasons

Cut and paste the matching words. Find letter pieces from page 127.

[bom]
Spring

[yeo-reum]
Summer

[ga-eul]
Autumn

[gyeo-ul]
Winter

리을 [ri-eul]

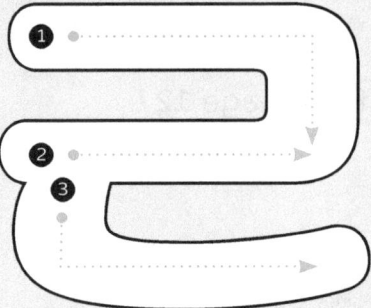

ROMANIZATION

[r/l]

라마 [ra-ma] **Llama**

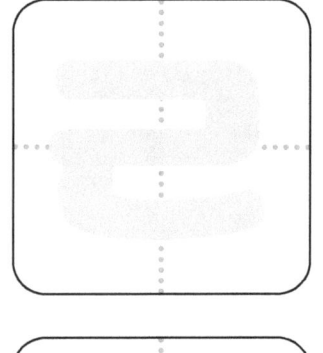 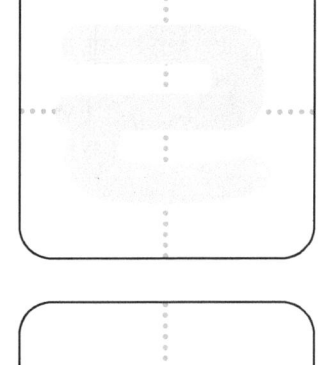 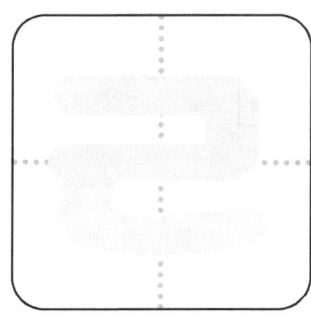 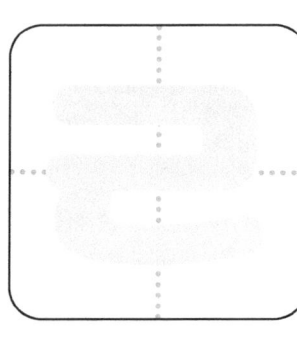

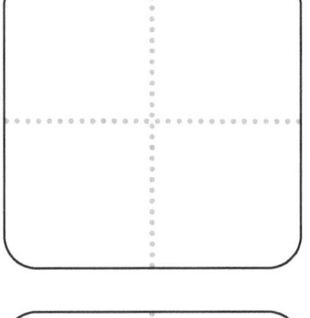 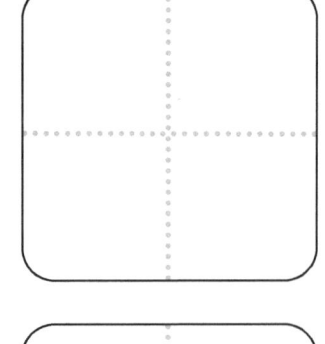 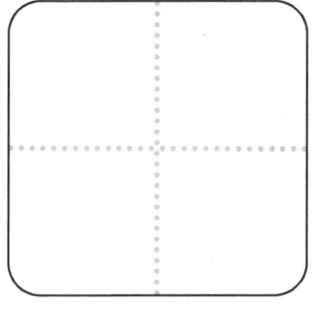 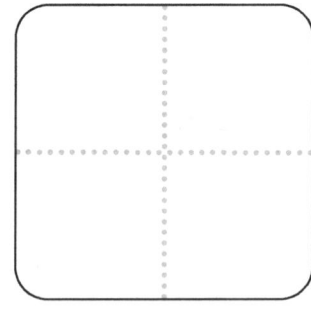

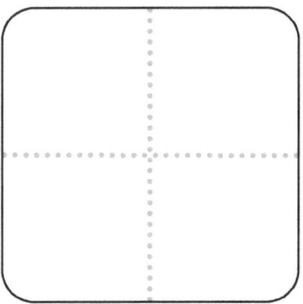 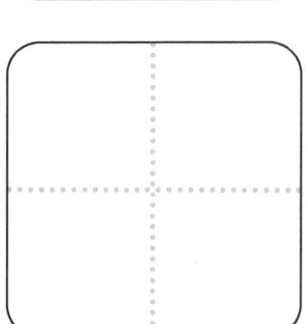 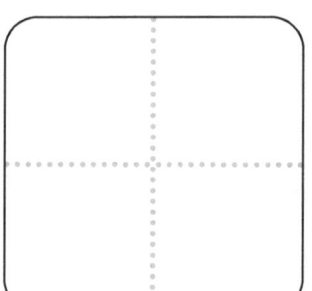 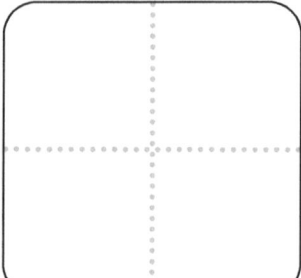

Color ㄹ

라면

[ra-myeon]

Ramen

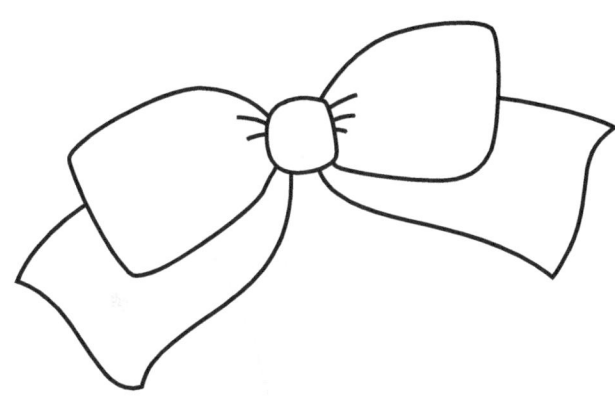

리본

[ri-bon]

Ribbon

런던

[reon-deon]

London

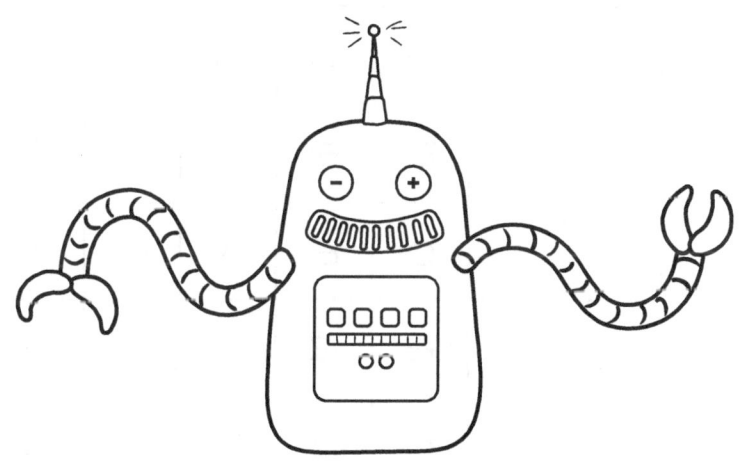

로봇

[ro-bot]

Robot

Find and Color

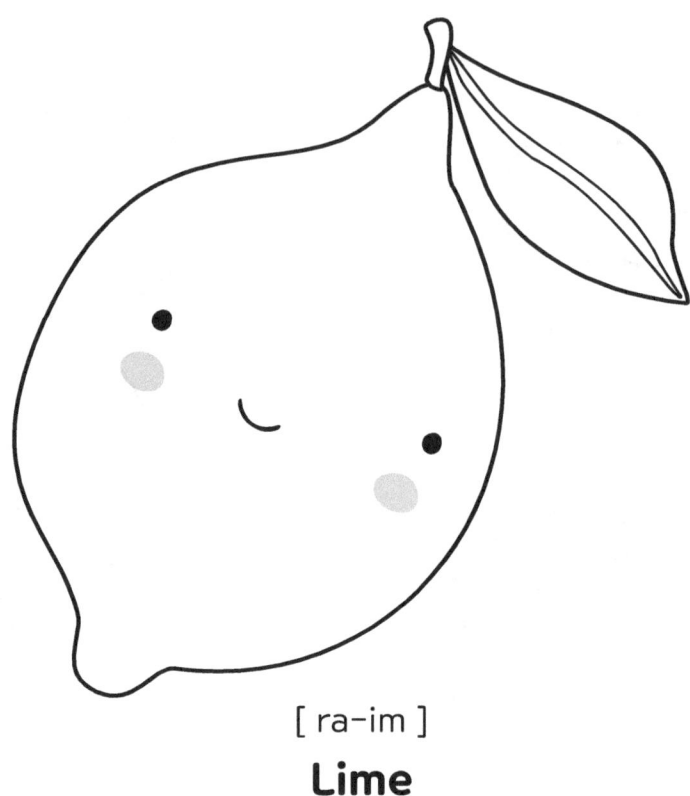

[ra-im]

Lime

ㄷ	ㄱ	ㅂ	ㄴ	ㅂ	ㄴ	ㅁ	ㅎ	ㄹ	ㄹ	ㅁ	ㅌ	ㄹ	ㅇ
ㅅ	ㅎ	ㄹ	ㄹ	ㄱ	ㄹ	ㅊ	ㅎ	ㄹ	ㅁ	ㅎ	ㄱ	ㄹ	ㄷ
ㅂ	ㅊ	ㅇ	ㄹ	ㅅ	ㄹ	ㅈ	ㅅ	ㄹ	ㅅ	ㄹ	ㅋ	ㄹ	ㅌ
ㄴ	ㄹ	ㄹ	ㄹ	ㄱ	ㄹ	ㄹ	ㄱ	ㅍ	ㄹ	ㄴ	ㅇ	ㄹ	ㅍ
ㅁ	ㄹ	ㄴ	ㅂ	ㅋ	ㄹ	ㅇ	ㅊ	ㅊ	ㅅ	ㄷ	ㅎ	ㅍ	ㅊ
ㅅ	ㄹ	ㄹ	ㄹ	ㄱ	ㄹ	ㅈ	ㅇ	ㄹ	ㄹ	ㄹ	ㄹ	ㄹ	ㄴ
ㅂ	ㅌ	ㄴ	ㅇ	ㅊ	ㄹ	ㅍ	ㅅ	ㄹ	ㄷ	ㅈ	ㄱ	ㄹ	ㅍ
ㅎ	ㄱ	ㄷ	ㅌ	ㅇ	ㅊ	ㅅ	ㅇ	ㄹ	ㄹ	ㄹ	ㄹ	ㄹ	ㅋ

Let's Make a Sound!

Color the consonant and trace the letters.

Match Words with Pictures

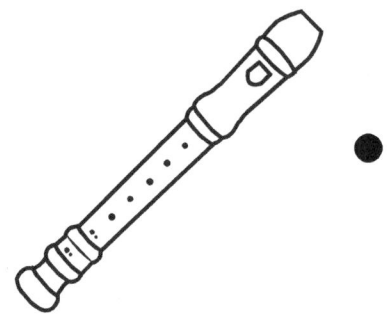

라디오
[ra-di-o]
Radio

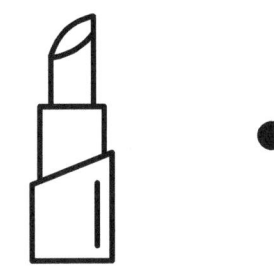

리코더
[ri-ko-deo]
Recorder

립스틱
[rip-seu-tik]
Lipstick

라이터
[ra-i-teo]
Lighter

Color By the Letters

러브

[reo-beu]

Love

라: 검정색 (Black) **랴:** 보라색 (Purple) **러:** 노란색 (Yellow) **로:** 빨간색 (Red)

료: 갈색 (Brown) **루:** 초록색 (Green) **르:** 회색 (Gray) **리:** 분홍색 (Pink)

Cut & Paste

Cut and paste the matching words and write it below. Find letter pieces from page 127.

로	마

[ro-ma]
Rome

로	프

[ro-peu]
Rope

루	비

[ru-bi]
Ruby

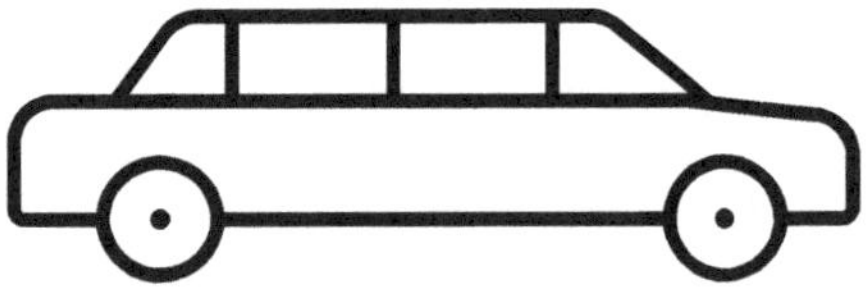

리	무	진

[ri-mu-jin]
Limousine

리	오	콘

[ri-mo-kon]
Remote Control

Vocabulary Builder

모양 | Shapes

Cut and paste the matching words. Find letter pieces from page 127.

[sa-gak-hyeong/ne-mo]
Square

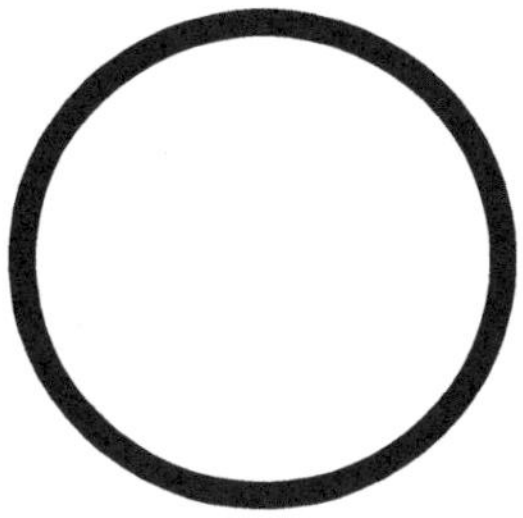

[won/dong-geu-ra-mi]
Circle

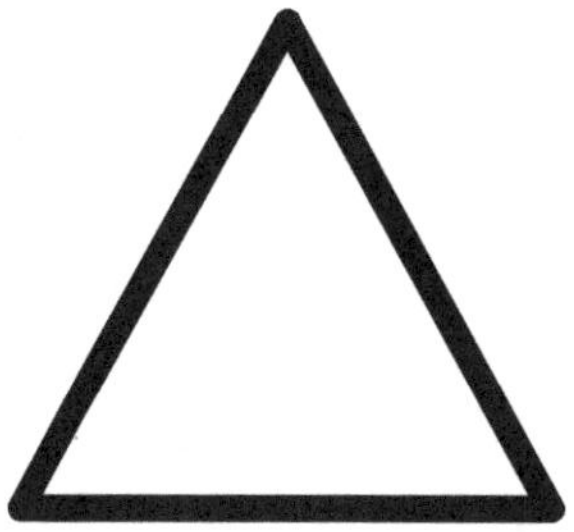

[sam-gak-hyeong/se-mo]
Triangle

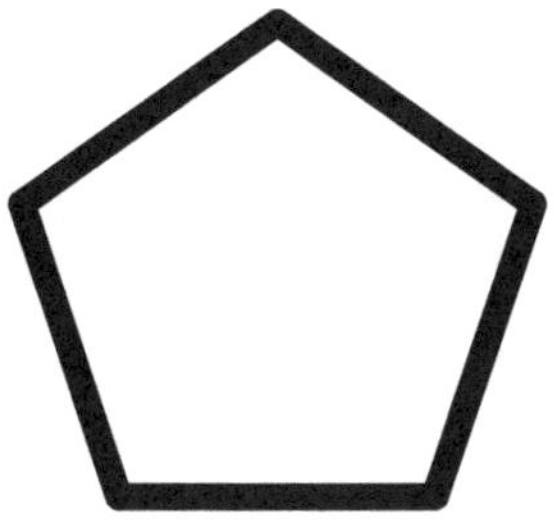

[o-gak-hyeong]
Pentagon

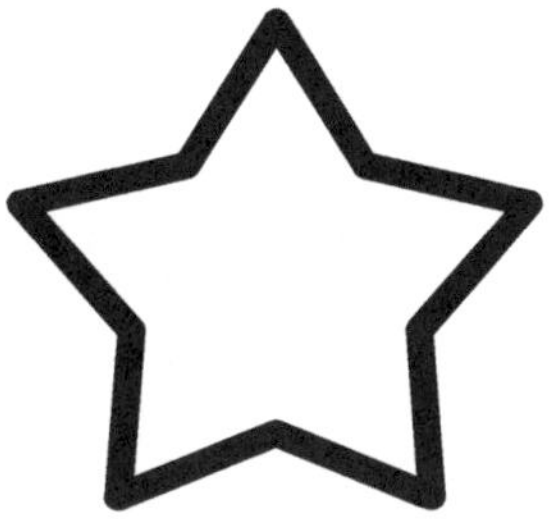

[byeol]
Star

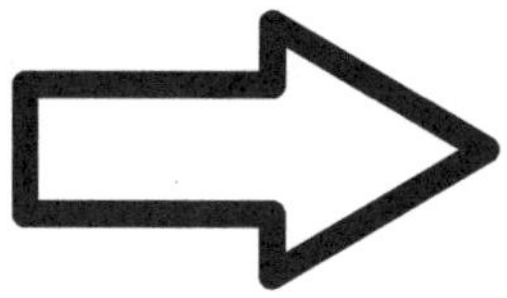

[hwa-sal-pyo]
Arrow

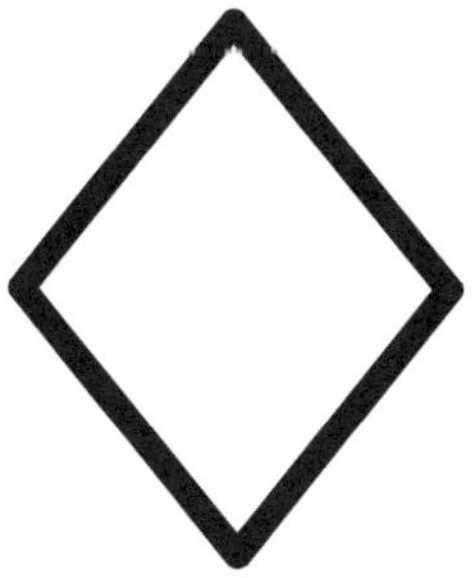

[ma-reum-mo]
Rhombus

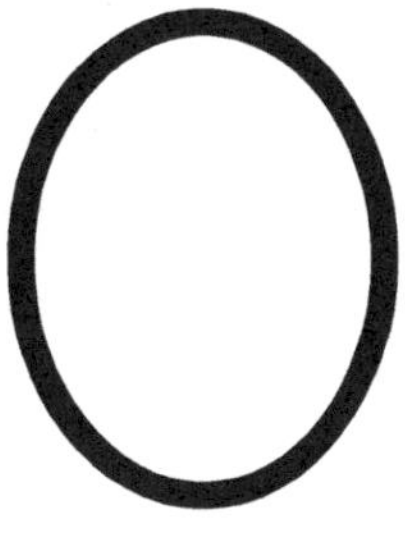

[ta-won]
Oval

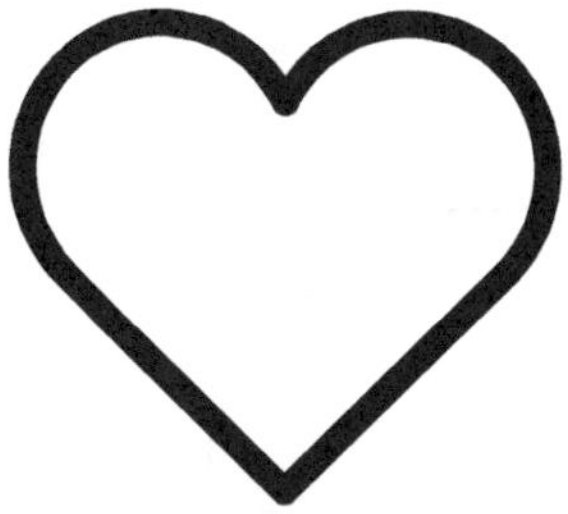

[ha-teu]
Heart

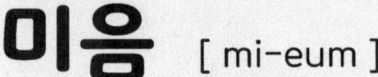

미음 [mi-eum]

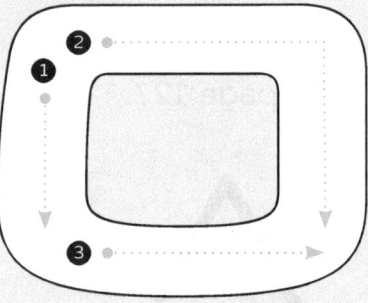

ROMANIZATION

[m]

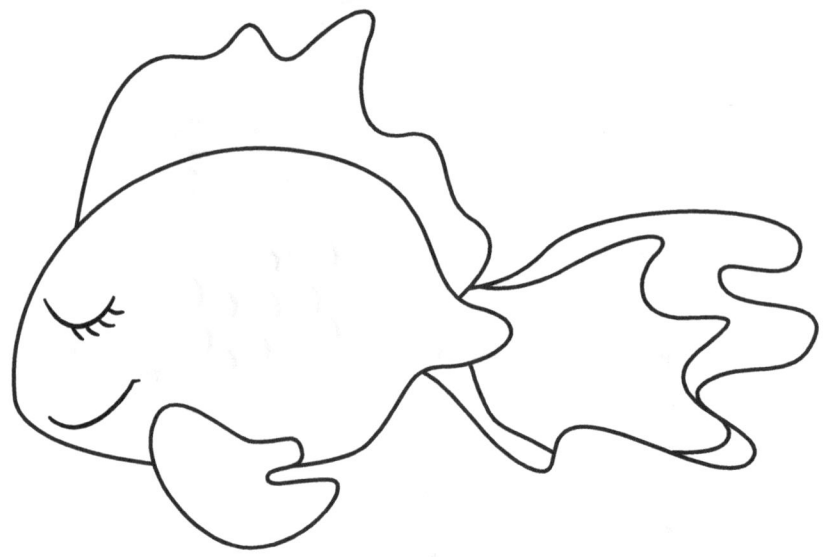

물고기 [mul-go-gi] **Fish**

Color

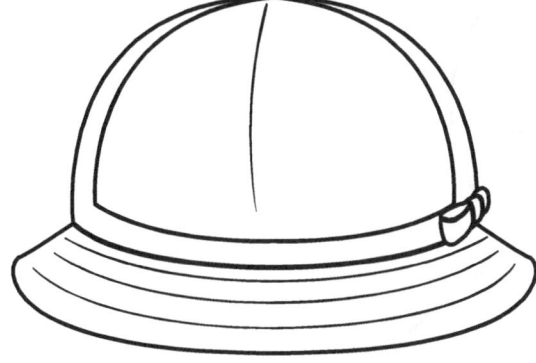

오 자

[mo-ja]

Hat

머 리

[meo-ri]

Head

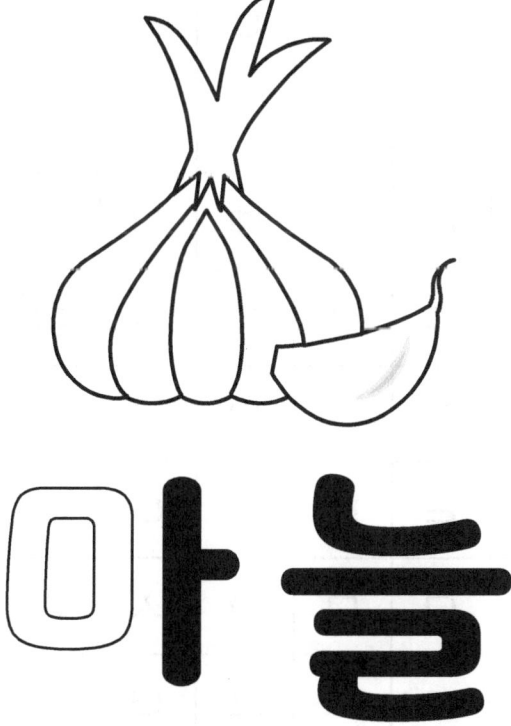

아 늘

[ma-neul]

Garlic

말

[mal]

Horse or Word/Speech

Find and Color

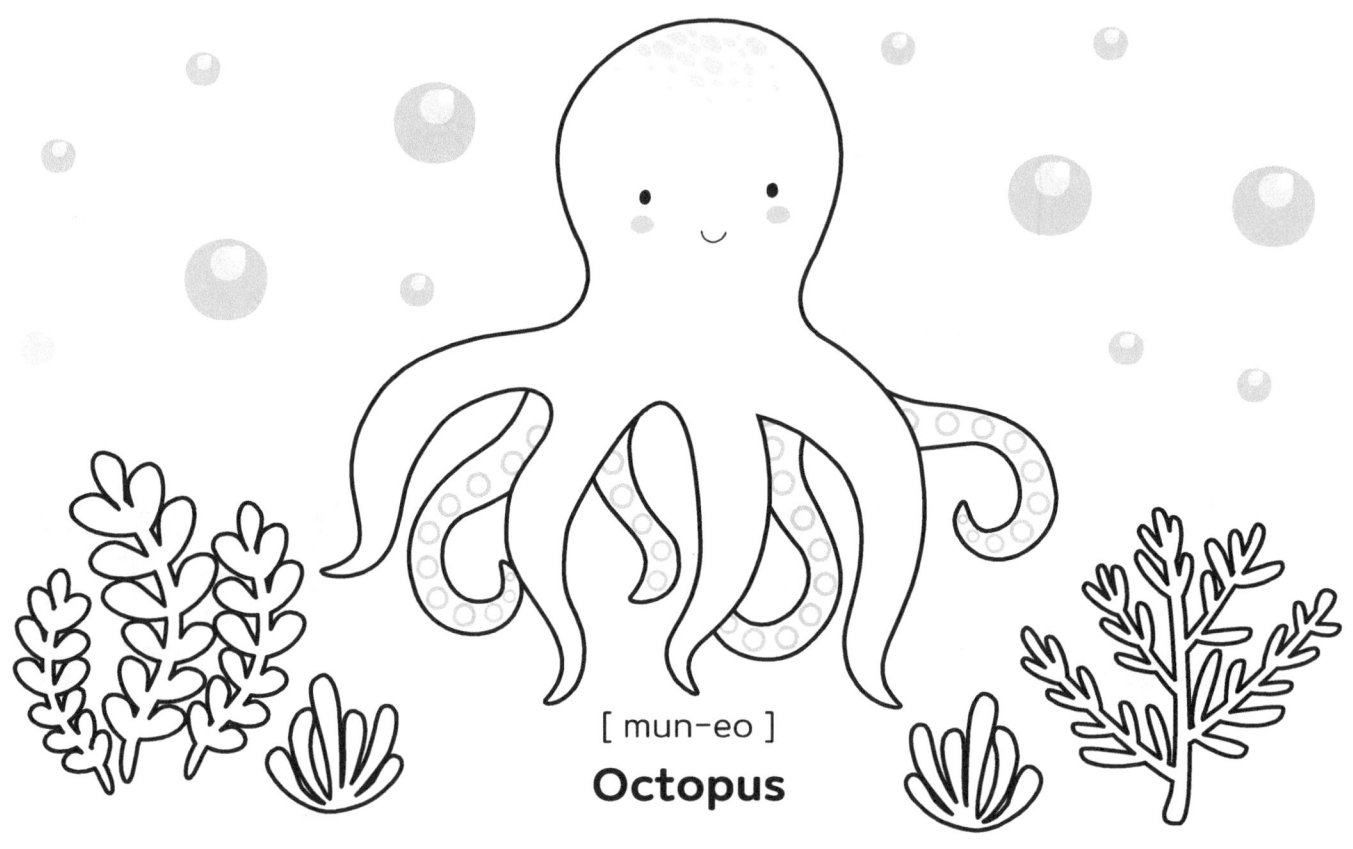

[mun-eo]

Octopus

ㄹ	ㅁ	ㅁ	ㅁ	ㅁ	ㅁ	ㅎ	ㅂ	ㄴ	ㄷ	ㄴ	ㅂ	ㅍ	ㅇ
ㅊ	ㅁ	ㄱ	ㄱ	ㄹ	ㅁ	ㅊ	ㅅ	ㅇ	ㅁ	ㄱ	ㄱ	ㄱ	ㅁ
ㅂ	ㅇ	ㅁ	ㅁ	ㅁ	ㅁ	ㅅ	ㅇ	ㄹ	ㄹ	ㅁ	ㅂ	ㄱ	ㅁ
ㅊ	ㅂ	ㅊ	ㄱ	ㅅ	ㄱ	ㄱ	ㅁ	ㄷ	ㅇ	ㅇ	ㅁ	ㅅ	ㅁ
ㅅ	ㅁ	ㅁ	ㅁ	ㅁ	ㅁ	ㅊ	ㅁ	ㄱ	ㄱ	ㅁ	ㄱ	ㄱ	ㅁ
ㄷ	ㅇ	ㅇ	ㅁ	ㄷ	ㄱ	ㅇ	ㅁ	ㄹ	ㄷ	ㅁ	ㄴ	ㅂ	ㅁ
ㅂ	ㅁ	ㅊ	ㄹ	ㄹ	ㄹ	ㅅ	ㅊ	ㅁ	ㄱ	ㅅ	ㅅ	ㅁ
ㅎ	ㅁ	ㅁ	ㅁ	ㅁ	ㅁ	ㅁ	ㄱ	ㄷ	ㄹ	ㅅ	ㅍ	ㅂ	ㅍ	ㅎ

Let's Make a Sound!

Color the consonant and trace the letters.

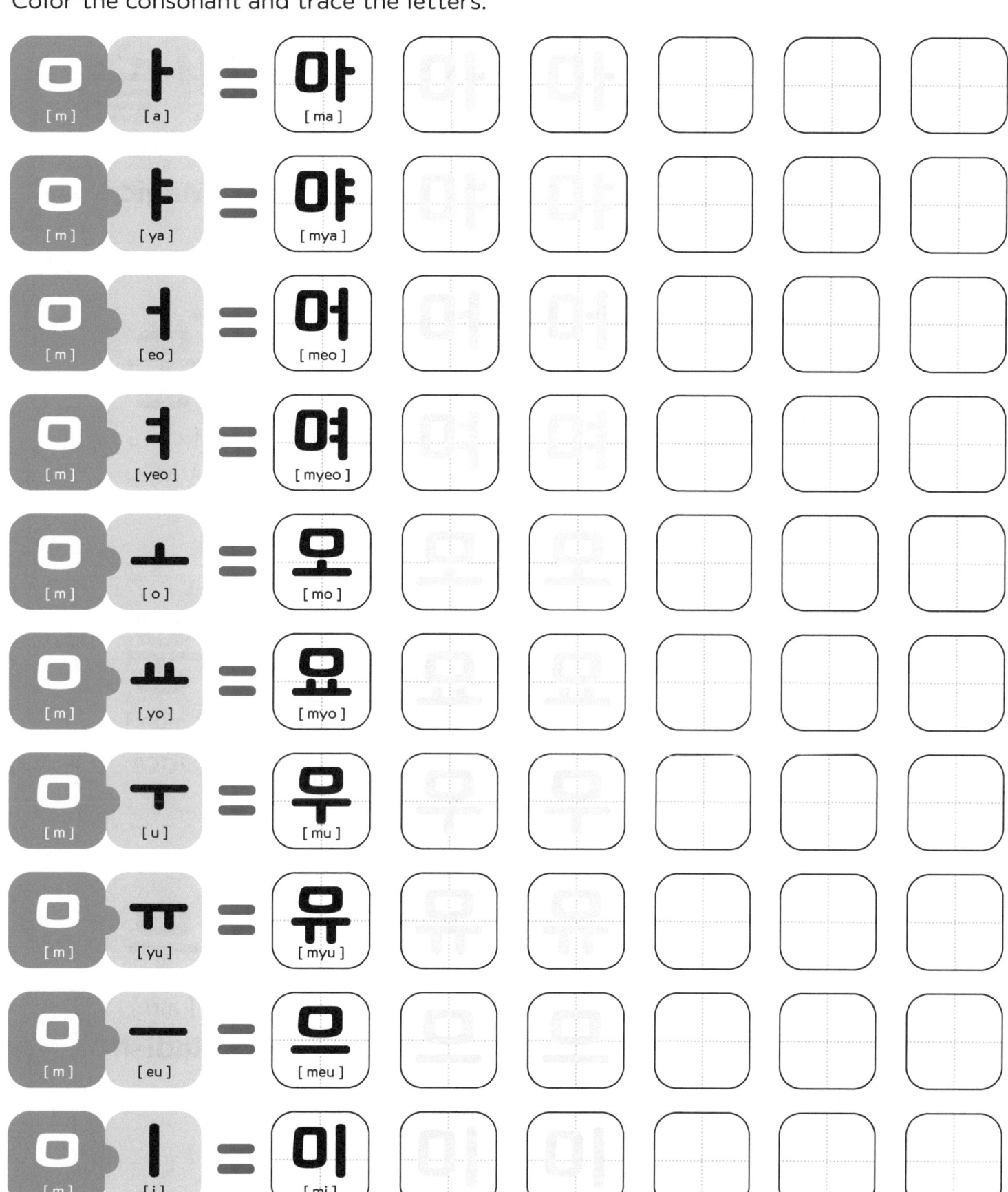

Match Words with Pictures

마술

[ma-sul]

Magic

물

[mul]

Water

문

[mun]

Door

우

[mu]

Radish

Color By the Letters

몬스터

[mon-seu-teo]

Monster

마: 빨간색 (Red)　**어:** 주황색 (Orange)　**모:** 노란색 (Yellow)　**묘:** 초록색 (Green)

무: 파란색 (Blue)　**므:** 보라색 (Purple)　**미:** 하늘색 (Light Blue)

Cut & Paste

Cut and paste the matching words and write it below. Find letter pieces from page 129.

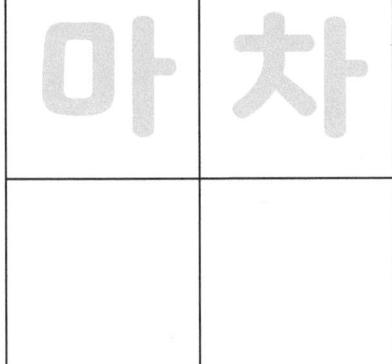

[ma-cha]
Carriage

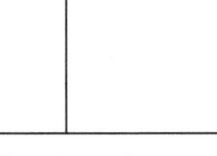

[mi-so]
Smile

[man-du]
Dumplings

[mo-gi]
Mosquitoes

[mi-sul]
Art

[mun-ja]
Writing System

요일 | Days of the Week

Cut and paste the matching words. Find letter pieces from page 129.

[wol-yo-il]	**Monday**
[hwa-yo-il]	**Tuesday**
[su-yo-il]	**Wednesday**
[mok-yo-il]	**Thursday**
[geum-yo-il]	**Friday**
[to-yo-il]	**Saturday**
[il-yo-il]	**Sunday**

비읍 [bi-eup]

1
2
3
4

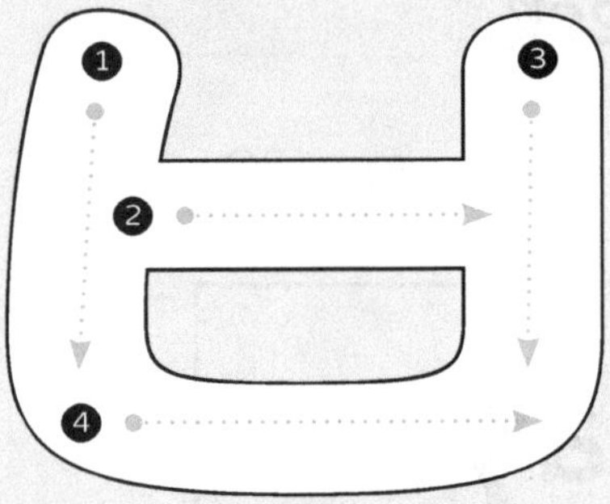

ROMANIZATION

[b/p]

벌 [beol] **Bee**

Color

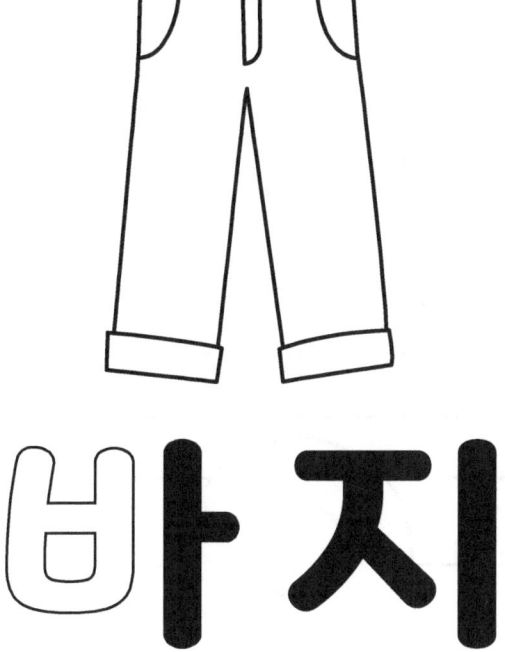

바지
[ba-ji]
Pants

버터
[beo-teo]
Butter

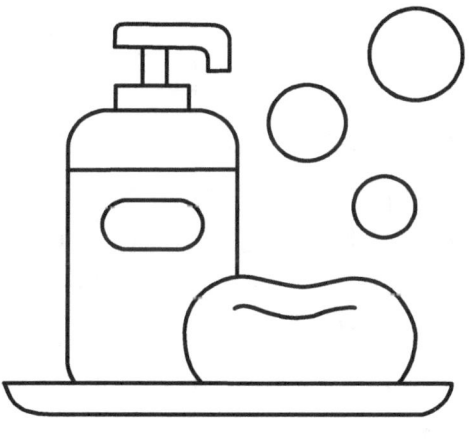

비누
[bi-nu]
Soap

버섯
[beo-seot]
Mushroom

Find and Color ㅂ

[beo-seu]

Bus

ㅅ	ㅎ	ㄱ	ㄴ	ㅅ	ㅁ	ㅋ	ㅎ	ㄹ	ㅇ	ㄹ	ㅈ	ㅌ	ㅅ	ㅊ
ㅂ	ㅊ	ㅂ	ㅎ	ㅊ	ㅂ	ㅊ	ㅊ	ㅁ	ㅊ	ㅂ	ㅊ	ㅇ	ㄷ
ㅂ	ㅍ	ㅂ	ㄷ	ㄴ	ㅂ	ㄷ	ㅌ	ㅇ	ㅂ	ㅇ	ㅂ	ㅇ	ㅍ
ㅂ	ㅂ	ㅂ	ㅁ	ㅂ	ㅂ	ㄱ	ㄴ	ㅂ	ㅊ	ㄱ	ㅊ	ㅂ	ㅊ
ㅂ	ㄷ	ㅂ	ㅅ	ㄷ	ㅂ	ㄷ	ㄹ	ㅂ	ㄷ	ㄴ	ㄷ	ㅂ	ㄷ
ㅂ	ㅂ	ㅂ	ㅊ	ㅁ	ㅂ	ㅌ	ㅁ	ㅈ	ㅍ	ㅈ	ㅌ	ㅊ	ㄹ
ㅍ	ㄷ	ㄴ	ㅌ	ㅋ	ㅂ	ㅇ	ㅂ	ㅂ	ㅂ	ㅂ	ㅂ	ㅂ	ㅂ
ㅎ	ㄱ	ㄹ	ㅇ	ㅅ	ㄴ	ㅁ	ㄱ	ㅅ	ㅌ	ㅁ	ㅇ	ㅎ	ㅅ

Let's Make a Sound!

Color the consonant and trace the letters.

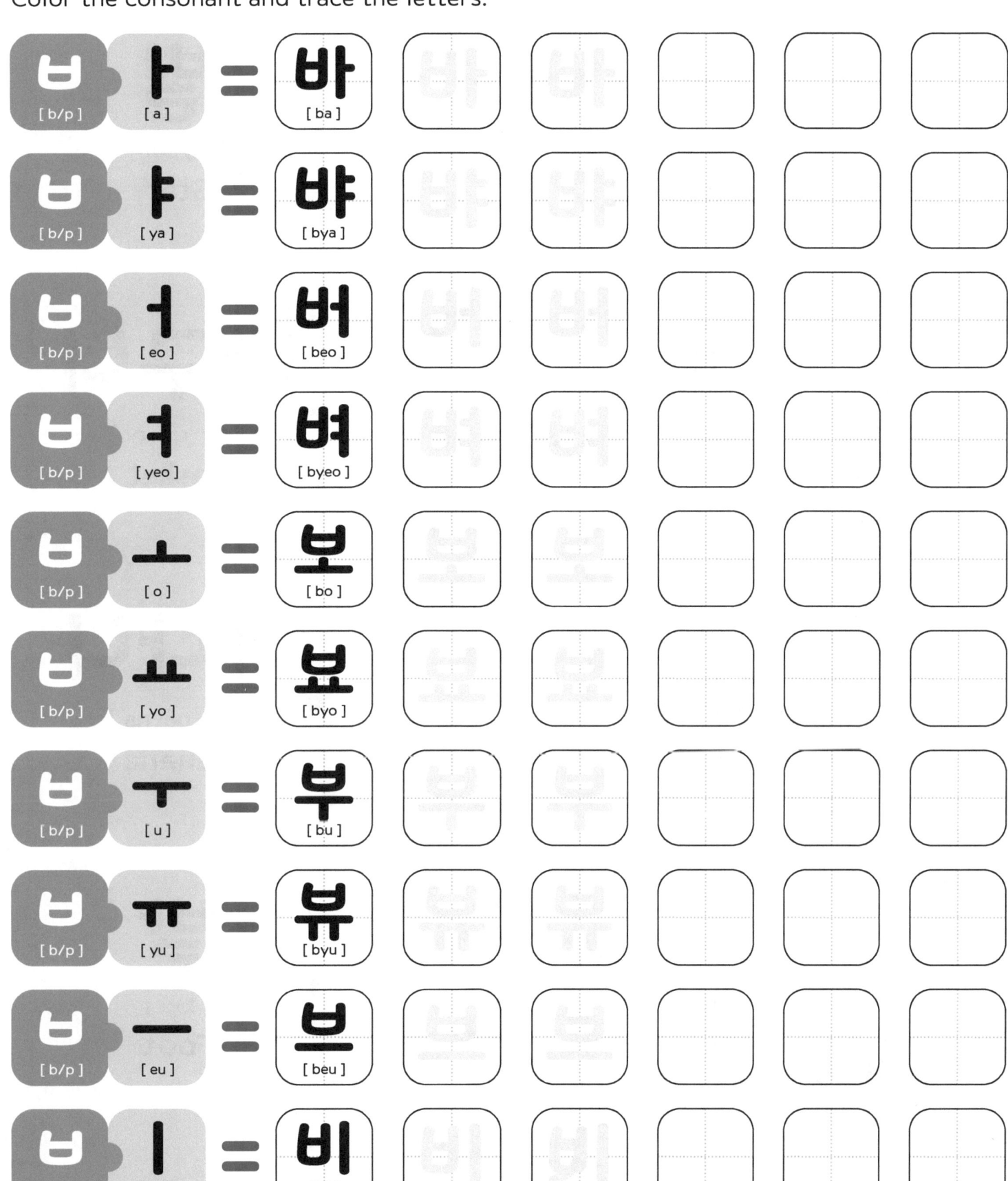

Match Words with Pictures

별
[byeol]
Star

바구니
[ba-gu-ni]
Basket

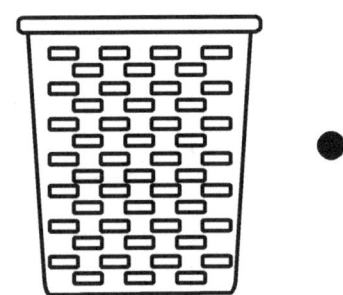

바나나
[ba-na-na]
Banana

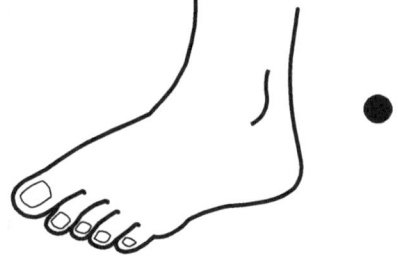

발
[bal]
Foot

Color By the Letters

부엉이
[bu-eong-i]
Owl

바: 갈색 (Brown) **버:** 노란색 (Yellow) **보:** 분홍색 (Pink)

부: 주황색 (Orange) **브:** 회색 (Gray) **비:** 검정색 (Black)

Cut & Paste

Cut and paste the matching words and write it below. Find letter pieces from page 129.

[ba-da]
Sea

[bul]
Fire

[ban-ji]
Ring

[bam]
Night or Chestnut

[bu-cheu]
Boots

[bi]
Rain

Vocabulary Builder

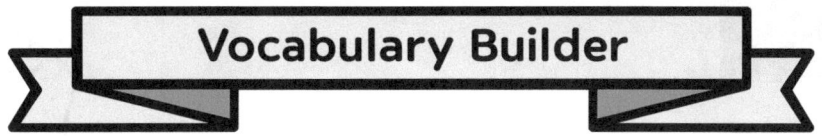

학용품 | School Supplies

Cut and paste the matching words. Find letter pieces from page 129.

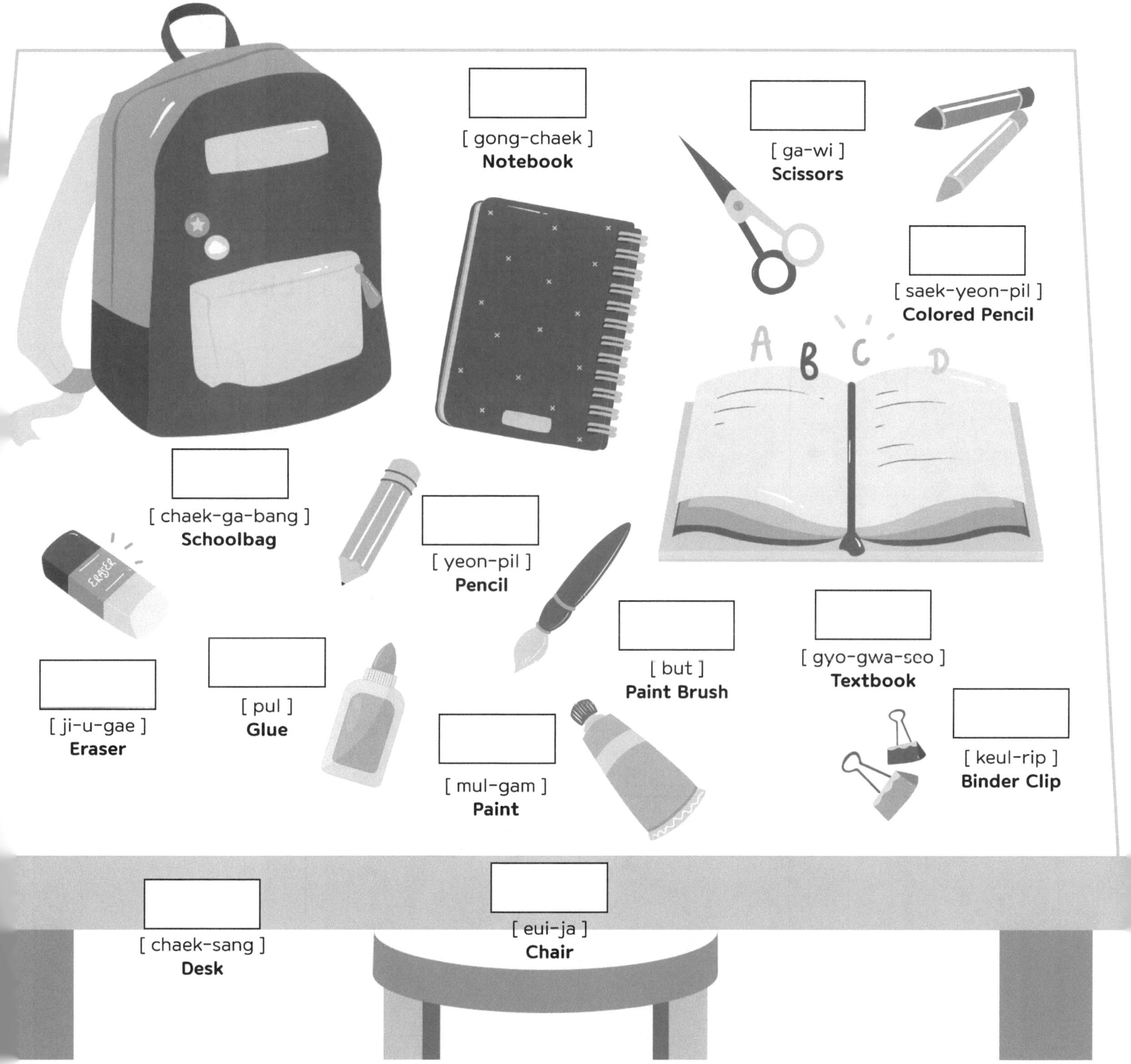
[gong-chaek]
Notebook
[ga-wi]
Scissors
[saek-yeon-pil]
Colored Pencil
A B C D
ERASER
[chaek-ga-bang]
Schoolbag
[yeon-pil]
Pencil
[but]
Paint Brush
[gyo-gwa-seo]
Textbook
[ji-u-gae]
Eraser
[pul]
Glue
[mul-gam]
Paint
[keul-rip]
Binder Clip
[chaek-sang]
Desk
[eui-ja]
Chair

시옷 [si-ot]

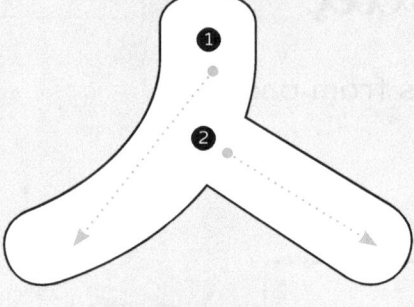

ROMANIZATION

[s]

사자 [sa-ja] **Lion**

Color

사탕
[sa-tang]
Candy

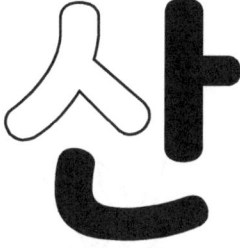

산
[san]
Mountain

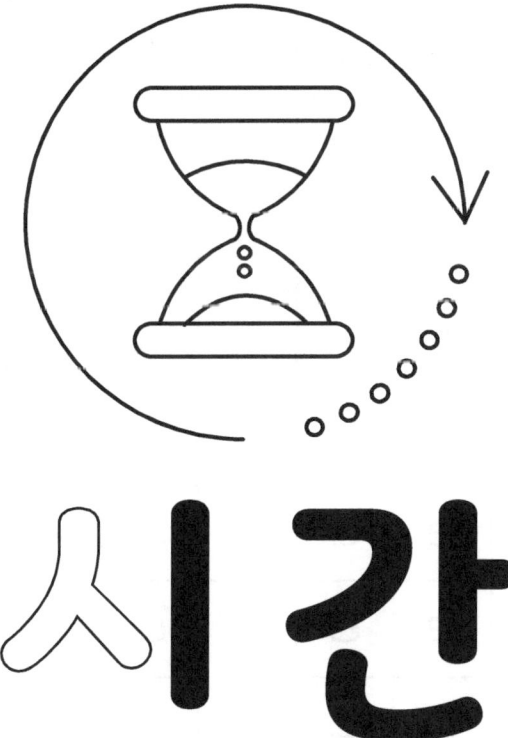

시간
[si-gan]
Time

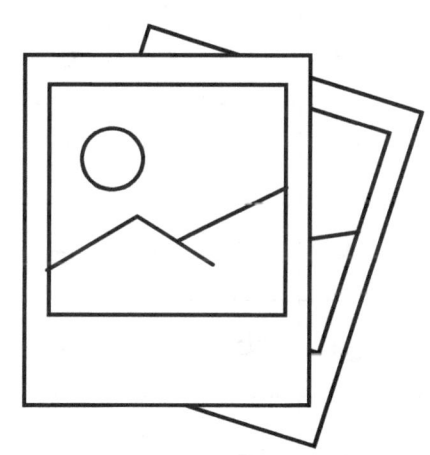

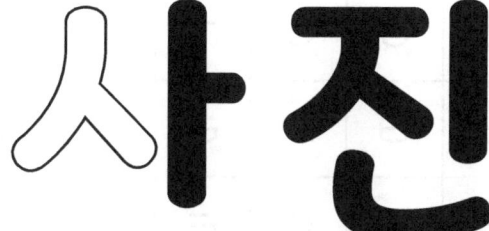

사진
[sa-jin]
Photo

Find and Color

[sa-seum]

Deer

ㄹ	ㅂ	ㅅ	ㅂ	ㄴ	ㄱ	ㅅ	ㅂ	ㄴ	ㄷ	ㄴ	ㅅ	ㅍ	ㅇ
ㅊ	ㄱ	ㅅ	ㄱ	ㄹ	ㅌ	ㅅ	ㅌ	ㄱ	ㄱ	ㅅ	ㄱ	ㅅ	ㅇ
ㅂ	ㅅ	ㄷ	ㅅ	ㅇ	ㄹ	ㅇ	ㅅ	ㅊ	ㄹ	ㄹ	ㅍ	ㅂ	ㄱ
ㅅ	ㅂ	ㅊ	ㄱ	ㅅ	ㄹ	ㅅ	ㅅ	ㄷ	ㅅ	ㅅ	ㅅ	ㅅ	ㅅ
ㅈ	ㄴ	ㅂ	ㄱ	ㅊ	ㅍ	ㅅ	ㅊ	ㄱ	ㅂ	ㅈ	ㄱ	ㄷ	ㅎ
ㄷ	ㅇ	ㅇ	ㄱ	ㄷ	ㄱ	ㅅ	ㄷ	ㄹ	ㄷ	ㅅ	ㅅ	ㅅ	ㄴ
ㅂ	ㅂ	ㅊ	ㄹ	ㄹ	ㄹ	ㅅ	ㅊ	ㄹ	ㅂ	ㅅ	ㄴ	ㅅ	ㅍ
ㅎ	ㄷ	ㅇ	ㅌ	ㅊ	ㅈ	ㅇ	ㄷ	ㄹ	ㄴ	ㅅ	ㅅ	ㅎ	

Let's Make a Sound!

Color the consonant and trace the letters.

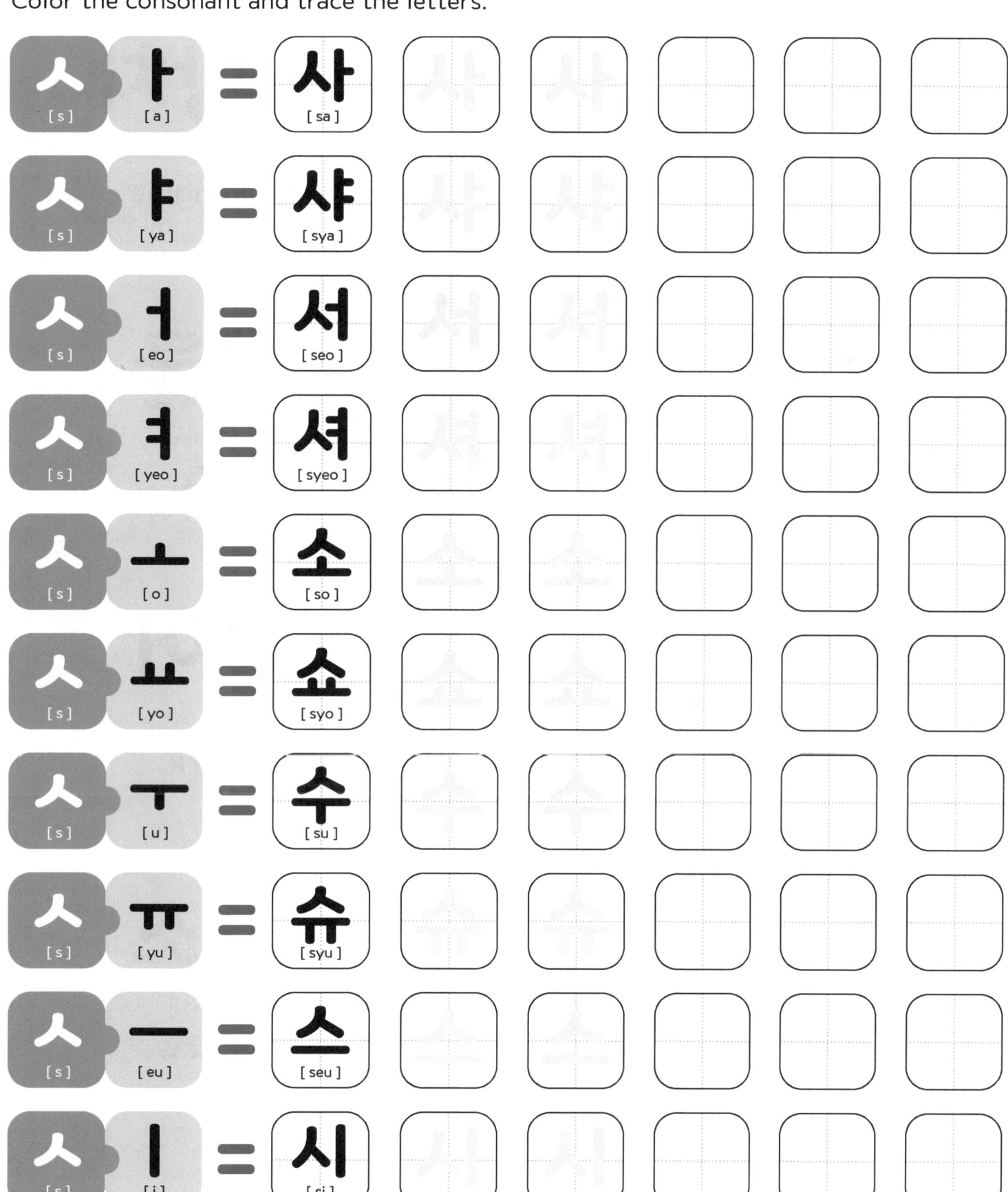

ㅅ [s] + ㅏ [a] = 사 [sa]

ㅅ [s] + ㅑ [ya] = 샤 [sya]

ㅅ [s] + ㅓ [eo] = 서 [seo]

ㅅ [s] + ㅕ [yeo] = 셔 [syeo]

ㅅ [s] + ㅗ [o] = 소 [so]

ㅅ [s] + ㅛ [yo] = 쇼 [syo]

ㅅ [s] + ㅜ [u] = 수 [su]

ㅅ [s] + ㅠ [yu] = 슈 [syu]

ㅅ [s] + ㅡ [eu] = 스 [seu]

ㅅ [s] + ㅣ [i] = 시 [si]

Match Words with Pictures

소방차

[so-bang-cha]

Fire Engine

선물

[seon-mul]

Gift

상어

[sang-eo]

Shark

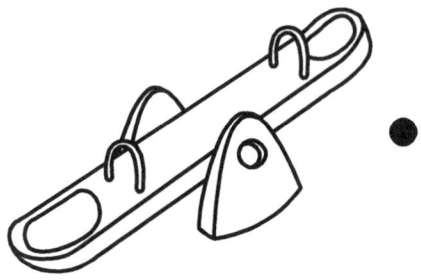

시소

[si-so]

Seesaw

Color By the Letters

소녀

[so-nyeo]
Little Girl

사: 머리색 (Any hair colors) **서:** 노란색 (Yellow) **소:** 빨간색 (Red)
쇼: 피부색 (Any skin colors) **수:** 초록색 (Green) **슈:** 하늘색 (Light Blue)
스: 보라색 (Purple) **시:** 분홍색 (Pink)

Cut & Paste

Cut and paste the matching words and write it below. Find letter pieces from page 131.

소

[so]
Cow

사 랑

[sa-rang]
Love

서 울

[seo-ul]
Seoul

Capital of South Korea

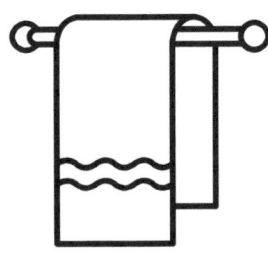

수 건

[su-geon]
Towel

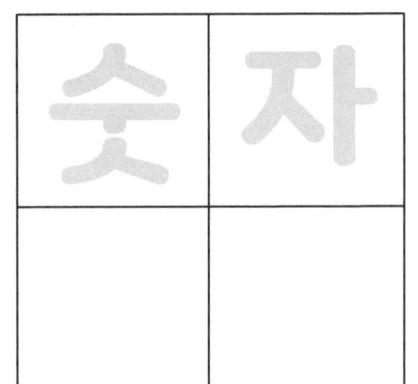

숫 자

[sut-ja]
Numbers

수 박

[su-bak]
Watermelon

옷과 장신구 | Clothing & Accessories

Cut and paste the matching words. Find letter pieces from page 131.

[ban-ba-ji]
Shorts

[mok-do-ri]
Scarf

[seu-we-teo]
Sweater

[mo-ja]
Hat

[yang-mal]
Socks

[jang-gap]
Gloves

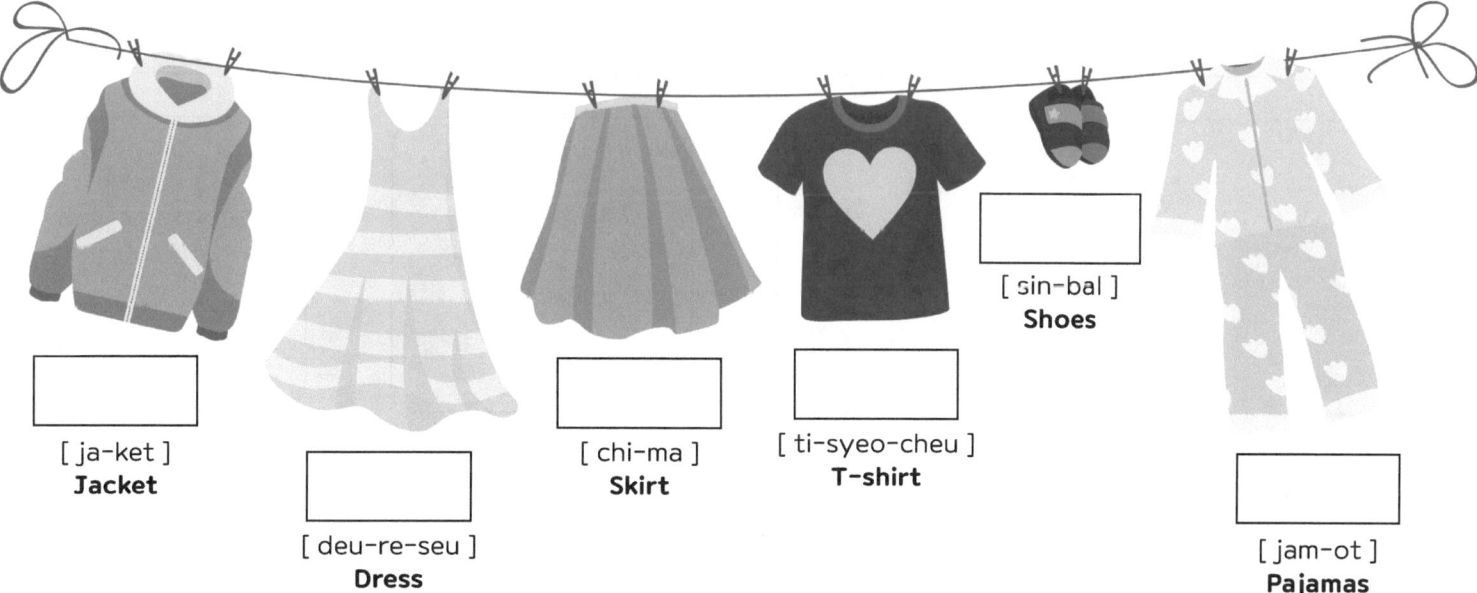

[ja-ket]
Jacket

[deu-re-seu]
Dress

[chi-ma]
Skirt

[ti-syeo-cheu]
T-shirt

[sin-bal]
Shoes

[jam-ot]
Pajamas

이응 [i-eung]

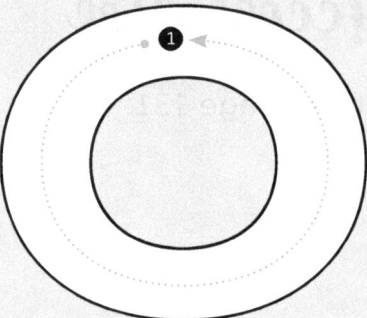

ROMANIZATION

[no sound/ng]

아기 [a-gi] **Baby**

Color

엉아

[eom-ma]

Mom

아빠

[a-ppa]

Dad

오빠

[o-ppa]

Older Brother*

*A younger female to call an older male or sibling

언니

[eon-ni]

Older Sister*

*A younger female to call an older female or sibling

Find and Color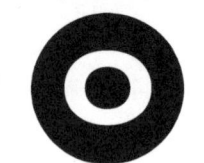

[o-ri]
Duck

ㄹ	ㄱ	ㅇ	ㅇ	ㅇ	ㅍ	ㅎ	ㅇ	ㅇ	ㅇ	ㅇ	ㅂ	ㅇ	ㅍ
ㄴ	ㅇ	ㄱ	ㅂ	ㄹ	ㅇ	ㅊ	ㅅ	ㄱ	ㄷ	ㅇ	ㄱ	ㅇ	ㅎ
ㄷ	ㅇ	ㅅ	ㅈ	ㄹ	ㅇ	ㄴ	ㅊ	ㄴ	ㄹ	ㅇ	ㅈ	ㅇ	ㄱ
ㄹ	ㅇ	ㅊ	ㅊ	ㅅ	ㅇ	ㄱ	ㅇ	ㅇ	ㅇ	ㅇ	ㅊ	ㅇ	ㄷ
ㅅ	ㅁ	ㅇ	ㅇ	ㅇ	ㅎ	ㅊ	ㅇ	ㅁ	ㄱ	ㄱ	ㅌ	ㅇ	ㄹ
ㄷ	ㅌ	ㄹ	ㄱ	ㄷ	ㄱ	ㅅ	ㅇ	ㄹ	ㅂ	ㅅ	ㄴ	ㅇ	ㅂ
ㅂ	ㅋ	ㅌ	ㅇ	ㅍ	ㅎ	ㅅ	ㅇ	ㅇ	ㅇ	ㅇ	ㅅ	ㅇ	ㅅ
ㅎ	ㅇ	ㅇ	ㅇ	ㅇ	ㅇ	ㄴ	ㄷ	ㄹ	ㅅ	ㅍ	ㅂ	ㅍ	ㅎ

Let's Make a Sound!

Color the consonant and trace the letters.

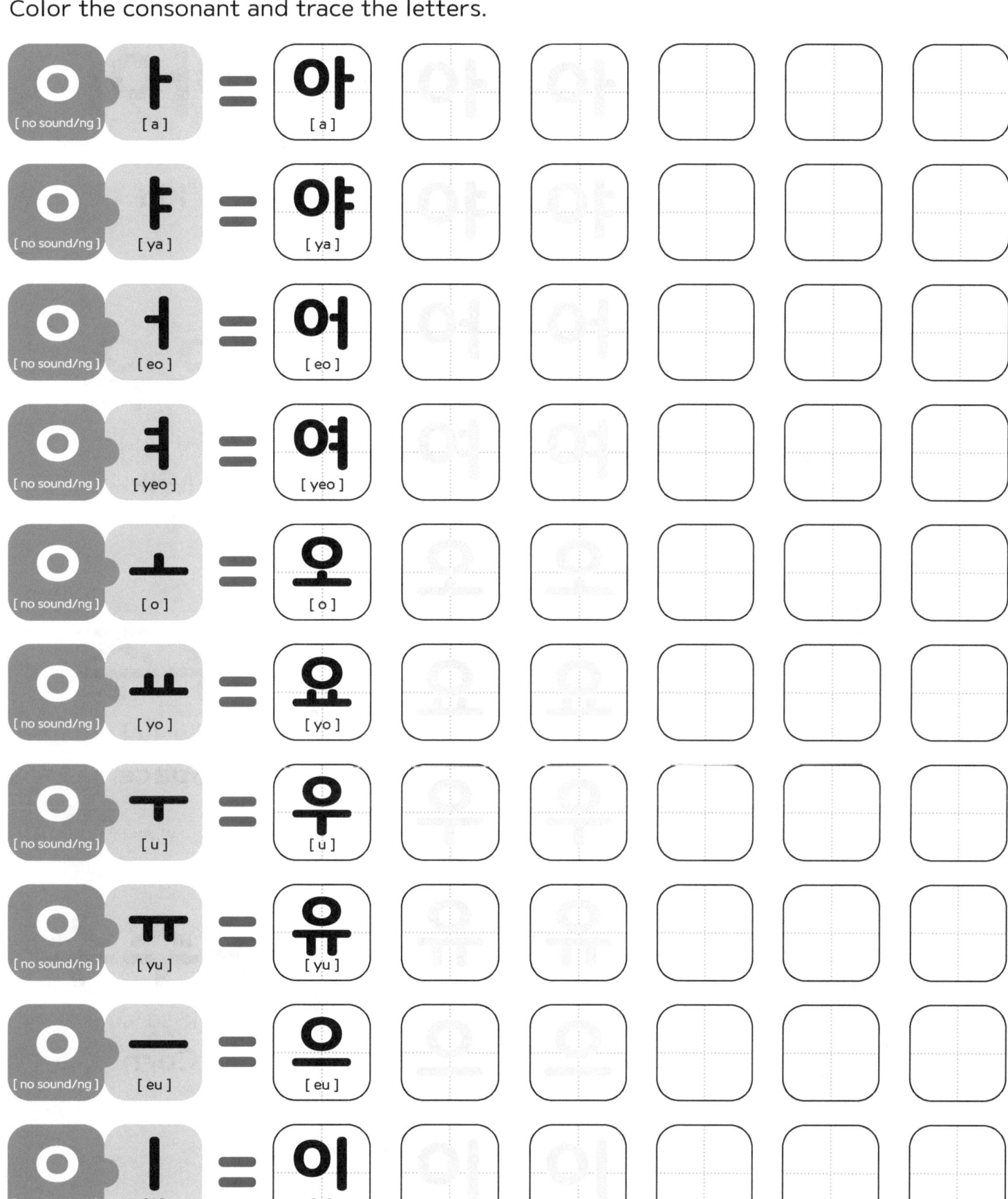

Match Words with Pictures

•

•
아이
[a-i]
Kid

•

•
우유
[u-yu]
Milk

•

•
우주
[u-ju]
Space

•

•
옥수수
[ok-su-su]
Corn

Color By the Letters

여우

[yeo-u]

Fox

아: 노란색 (Yellow)　**야:** 보라색 (Purple)　**어:** 빨간색 (Red)

여: 살색 (Peach)　**오:** 파란색 (Blue)　**우:** 초록색 (Green)　**으:** 분홍색 (Pink)

Cut & Paste

Cut and paste the matching words and write it below. Find letter pieces from page 131.

이 사

[i-sa]

Moving

오 이

[o-i]

Cucumber

어 부

[eo-bu]

Fisherman

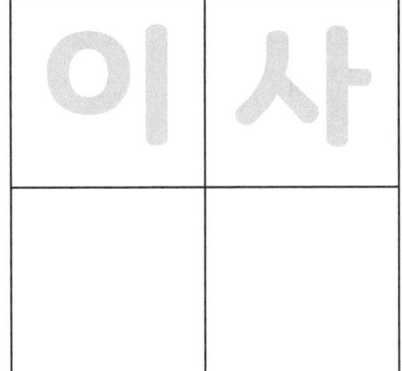

여 자

[yeo-ja]

Woman/Female

요 리

[yo-ri]

Cooking

유 성

[yu-seong]

Shooting Star

Vocabulary Builder

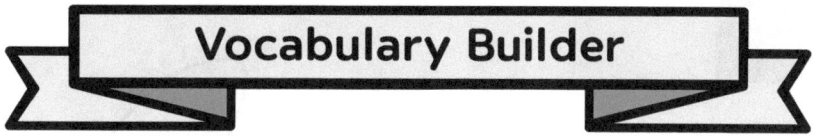

감정 | feelings

Cut and paste the matching words. Find letter pieces from page 131.

[seul-peun]
Sad

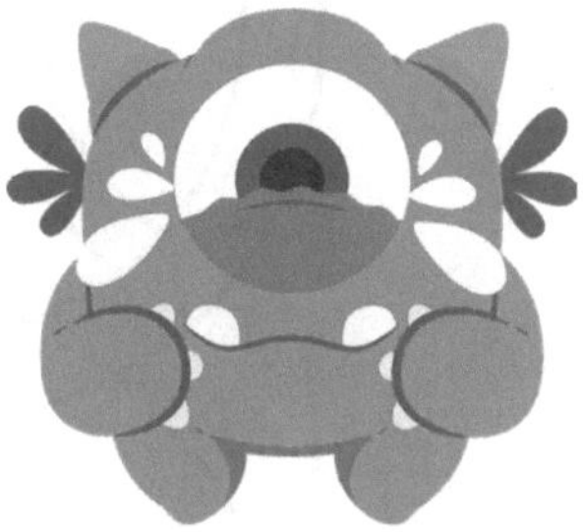

[hwa-nan]
Angry

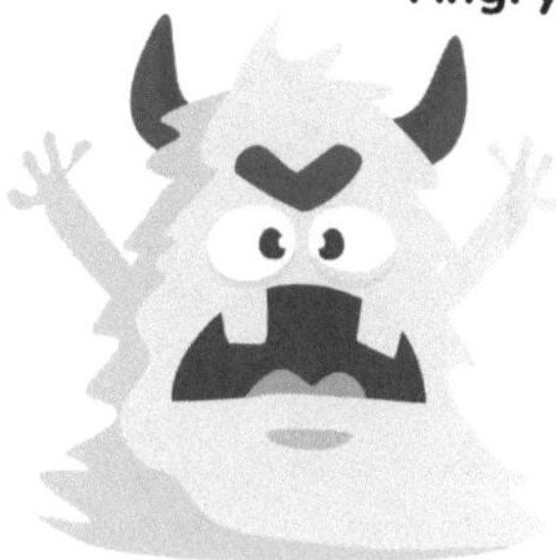

[gi-ppeun]
Happy

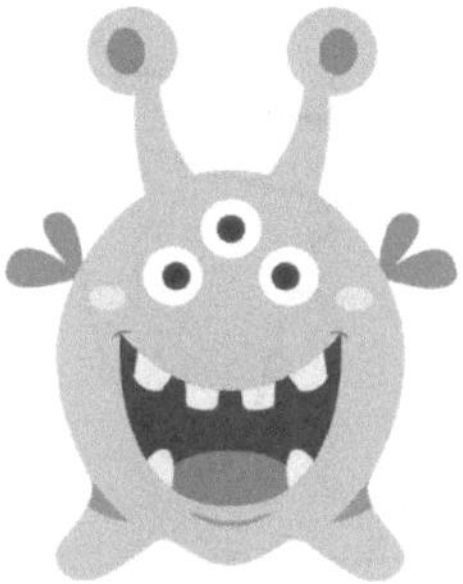

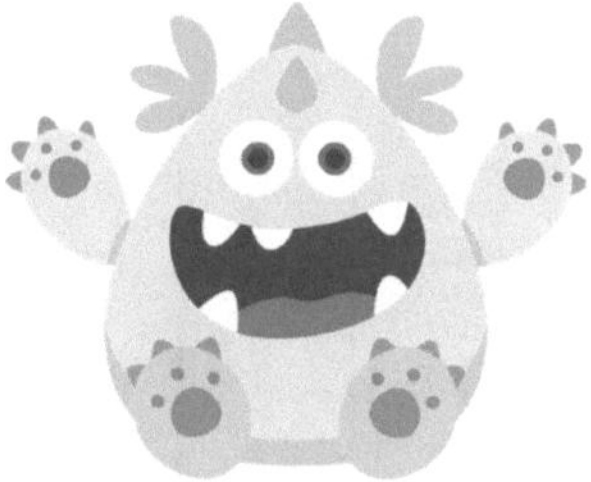

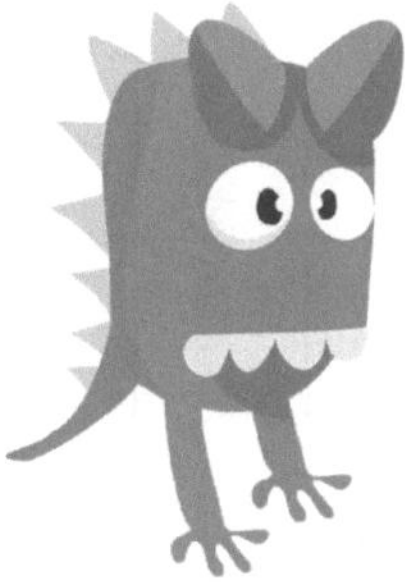

[ddeol-rin]
Nervous

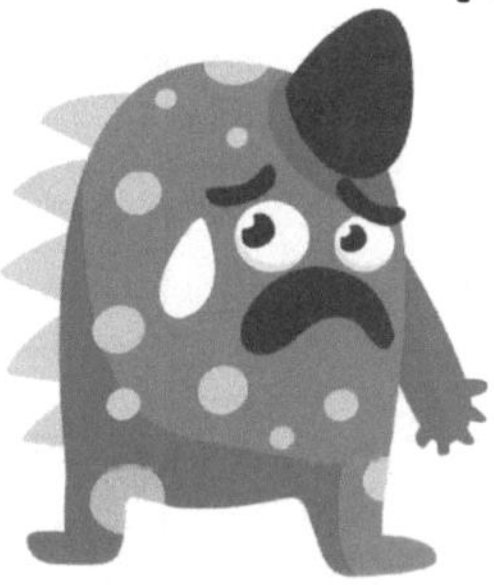

[heung-bun-doen]
Excited

[mu-seo-un]
Scared

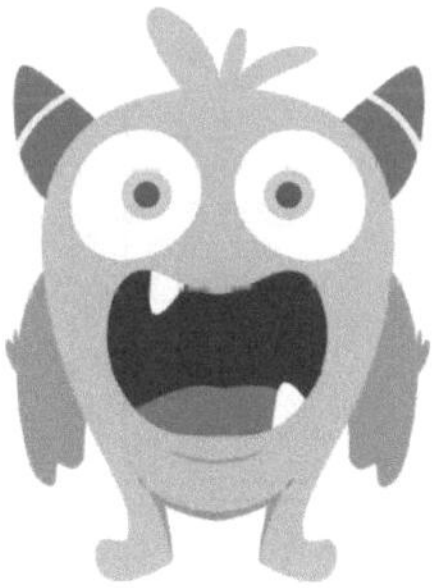

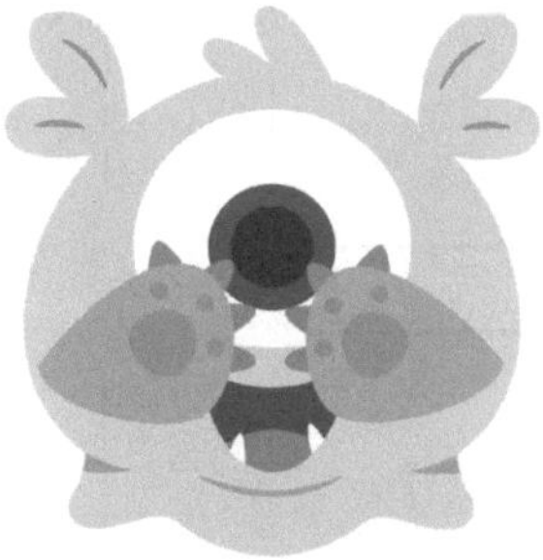

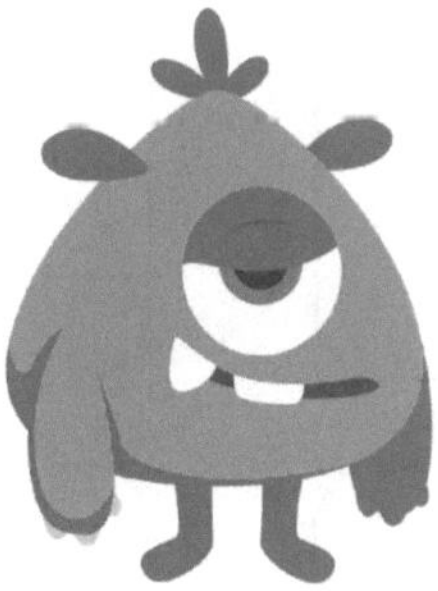

[nol-ran]
Surprised

[bu-kkeu-reo-un]
Embarrassed

[pi-gon-han]
Tired

지읒 [ji-eut]

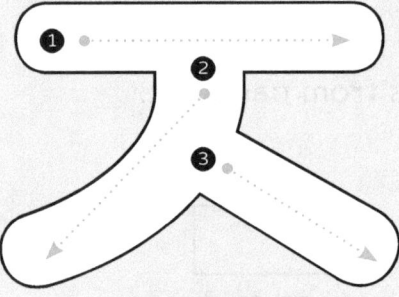

ROMANIZATION

[j]

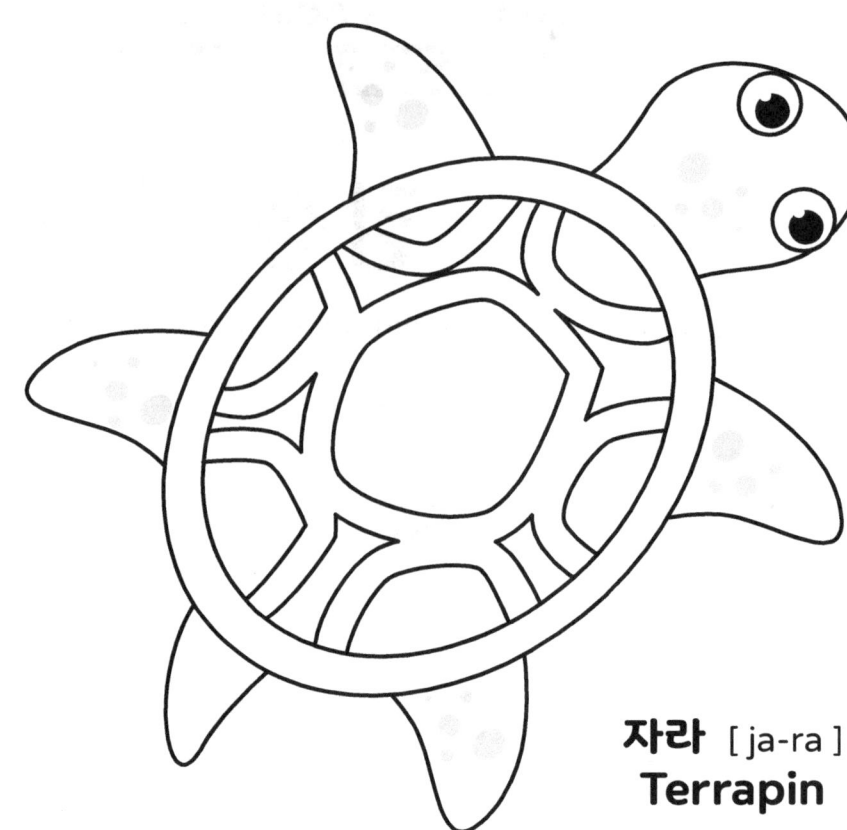

자라 [ja-ra]
Terrapin

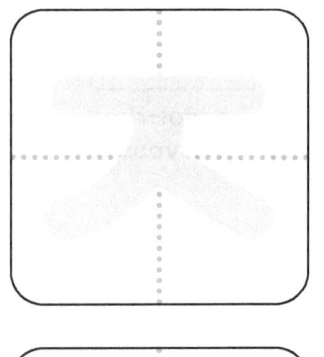 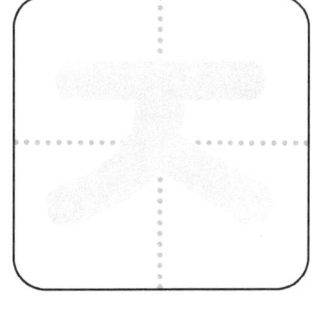 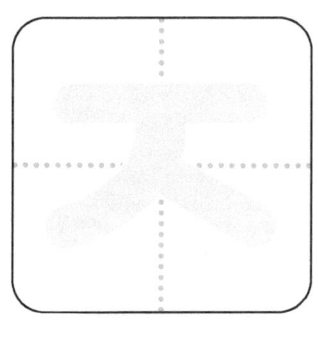 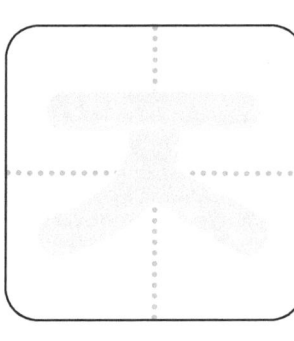

Color

[jang-mi]

Rose

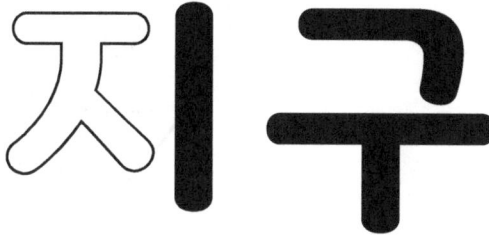

[ji-gu]

Earth

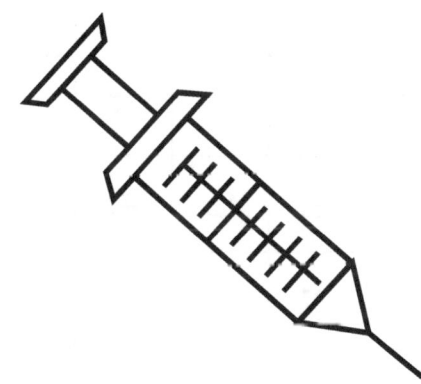

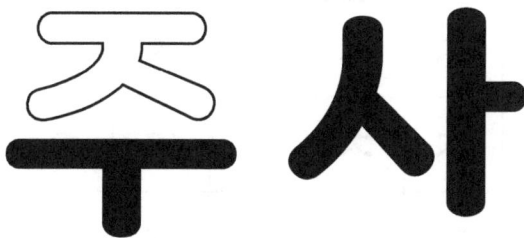

[ju-sa]

Shot

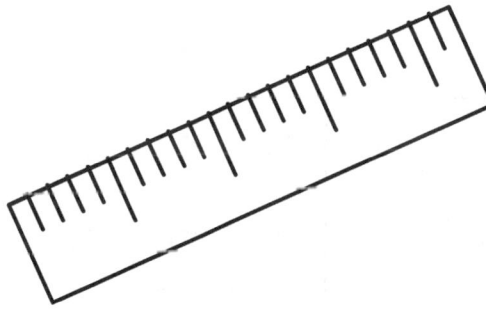

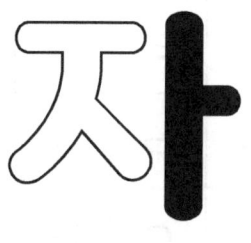

[ja]

Ruler

Find and Color ㅈ

[jeo-geum]
Saving

ㄹ	ㅅ	ㅌ	ㄱ	ㅍ	ㅈ	ㄹ	ㅅ	ㅈ	ㅈ	ㅈ	ㅈ	ㄹ	ㅇ
ㄷ	ㅈ	ㅈ	ㅈ	ㄷ	ㅈ	ㄷ	ㅍ	ㄹ	ㅇ	ㄷ	ㅈ	ㄷ	ㅍ
ㄴ	ㅌ	ㅈ	ㄷ	ㄴ	ㅈ	ㄴ	ㅌ	ㄴ	ㅌ	ㄴ	ㅋ	ㅅ	ㅇ
ㅁ	ㅇ	ㅈ	ㄱ	ㅈ	ㅈ	ㅁ	ㅈ	ㅈ	ㅈ	ㅈ	ㅈ	ㅈ	ㄱ
ㅊ	ㅈ	ㅇ	ㅈ	ㅊ	ㅈ	ㅇ	ㅂ	ㄹ	ㅇ	ㅊ	ㅂ	ㄹ	ㅂ
ㅋ	ㅈ	ㅌ	ㅈ	ㅋ	ㅈ	ㅋ	ㄴ	ㅈ	ㅈ	ㅈ	ㅈ	ㅋ	ㄴ
ㅂ	ㅊ	ㅂ	ㅊ	ㅇ	ㅈ	ㅂ	ㄹ	ㅈ	ㅊ	ㅂ	ㅈ	ㅇ	ㅊ
ㅎ	ㄷ	ㅇ	ㅌ	ㄹ	ㄷ	ㅍ	ㄷ	ㅈ	ㅈ	ㅈ	ㅈ	ㅎ	ㄷ

Let's Make a Sound!

Color the consonant and trace the letters.

Match Words with Pictures

잠자리
[jam-ja-ri]
Dragonfly

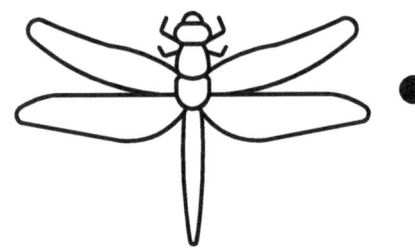

지렁이

[ji-reong-i]
Earthworm

집
[jip]
House

종
[jong]
Bell

Color By the Letters

자전거
[ja-jeon-geo]
Bicycle

자: 초록색 (Green) **샤:** 머리색 (Any hair colors) **저:** 피부색 (Any skin colors)

조: 회색 (Gray) **죠:** 검정색 (Black) **주:** 하늘색 (Light Blue) **쥬:** 빨간색 (Red)

즈: 보라색 (Purple) **지:** 분홍색 (Pink)

Cut & Paste

Cut and paste the matching words and write it below. Find letter pieces from page 133.

[ja-du]
Plum

[jeo-nyeok]
Evening

[jeo-ul]
Scale

[ji-do]
Map

[jam]
Sleep

[jang-nan-gam]
Toy

태양계 | Solar System

Cut and paste the matching words. Find letter pieces from page 133.

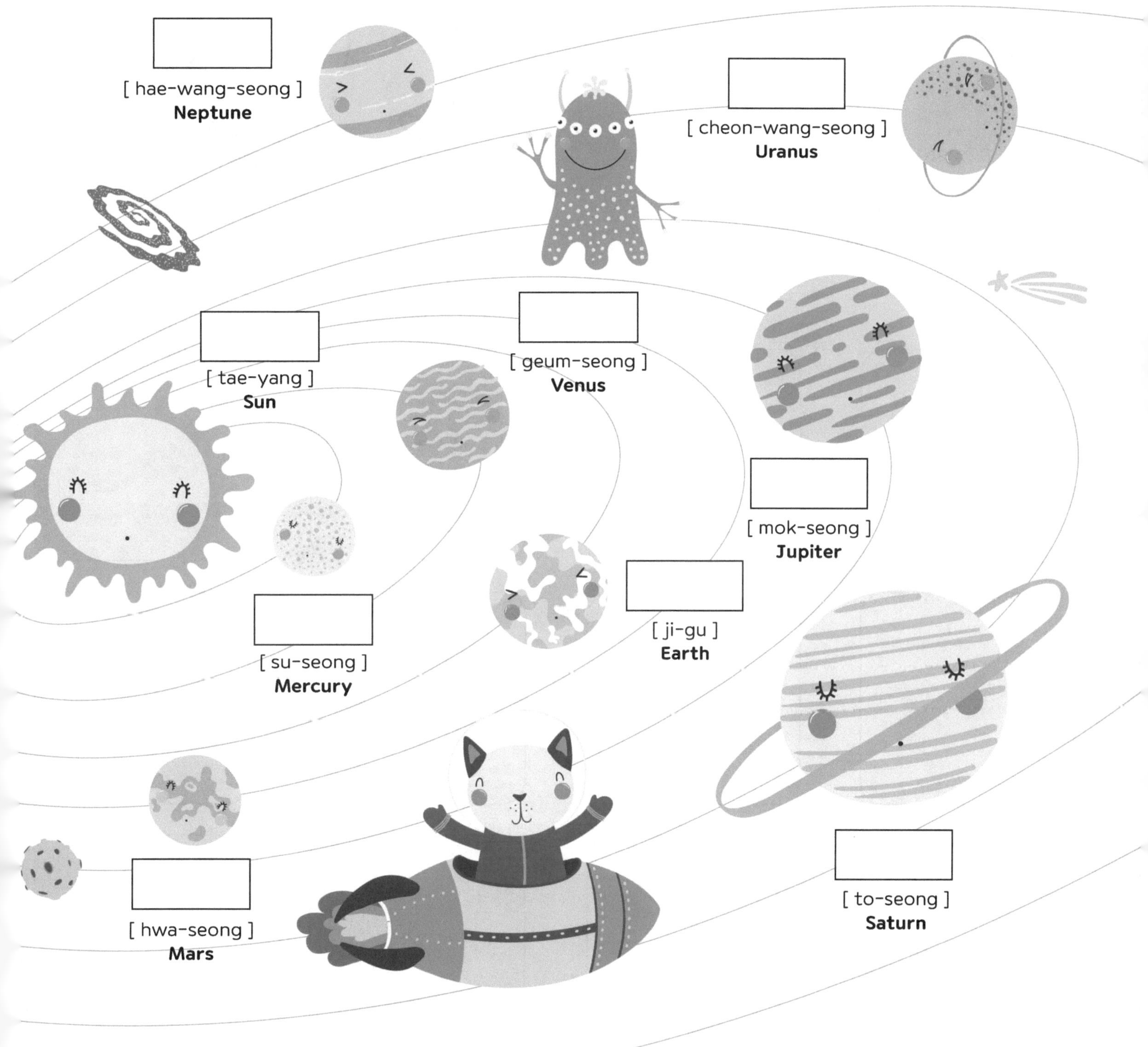

[hae-wang-seong]
Neptune

[cheon-wang-seong]
Uranus

[tae-yang]
Sun

[geum-seong]
Venus

[mok-seong]
Jupiter

[su-seong]
Mercury

[ji-gu]
Earth

[hwa-seong]
Mars

[to-seong]
Saturn

치읓 [chi-eut]

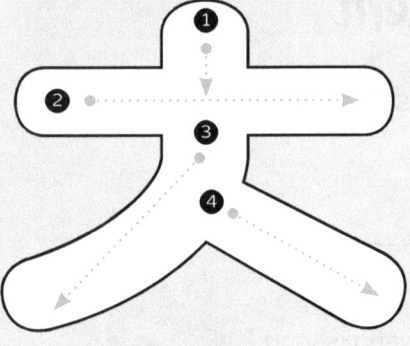

ROMANIZATION

[ch]

천사
[cheon-sa]
Angel

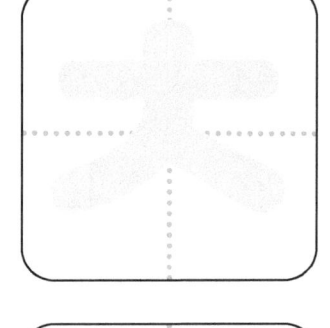
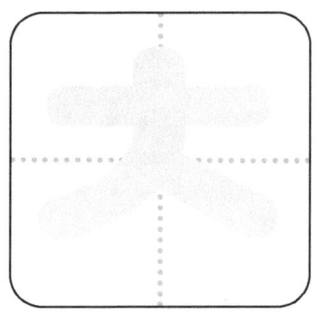
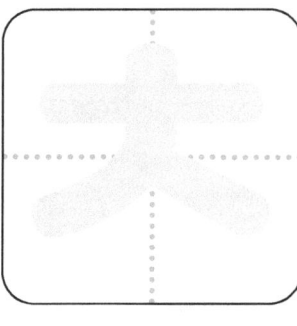

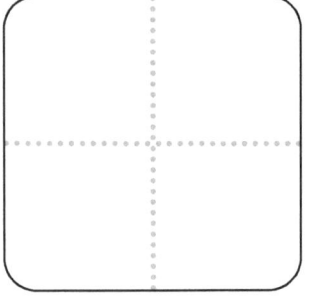
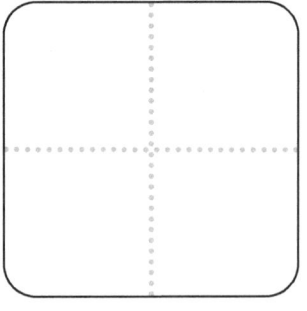
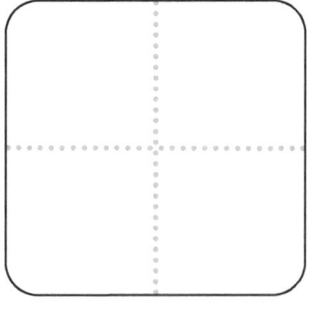
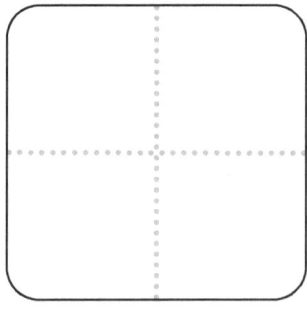

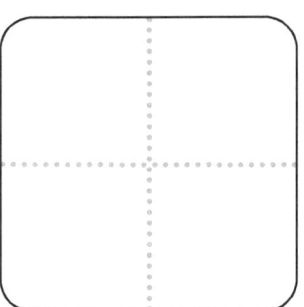
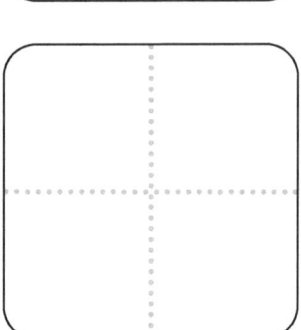
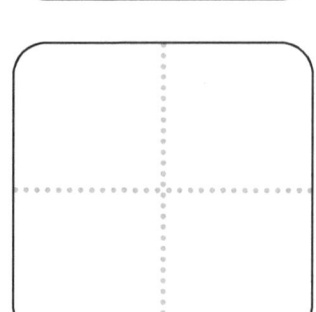

Color

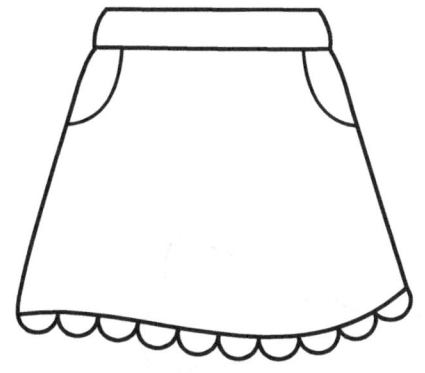

[chi-ma]

Skirt

치즈

[chi-jeu]

Cheese

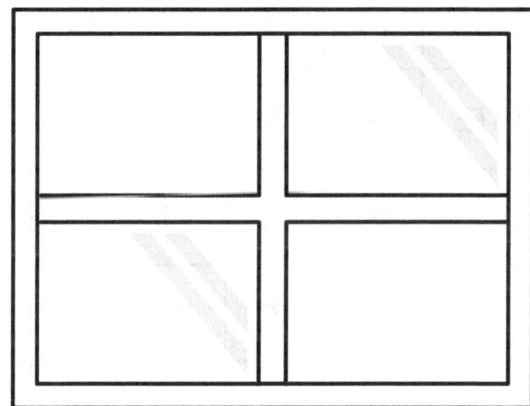

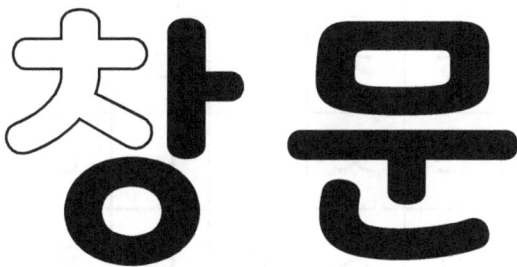

[chang-mun]

Window

친구

[chin-gu]

Friend

Find and Color 大

[cha]

Car

ㄹ	ㄹ	ㅂ	ㄴ	ㅅ	ㅊ	ㅂ	ㄴ	ㄷ	ㅇ	ㅊ	ㅍ	ㅂ	ㅁ	ㅇ
ㄷ	ㅅ	ㅊ	ㅊ	ㅊ	ㅊ	ㅊ	ㄹ	ㅌ	ㅊ	ㅅ	ㅈ	ㅍ	ㅌ
ㄱ	ㄹ	ㅌ	ㅇ	ㅊ	ㅎ	ㄱ	ㅅ	ㅎ	ㅊ	ㄱ	ㄱ	ㄱ	ㅎ
ㅂ	ㅇ	ㄴ	ㅂ	ㅊ	ㄱ	ㄹ	ㅂ	ㄴ	ㅊ	ㅊ	ㅊ	ㄹ	ㄴ
ㄴ	ㅋ	ㅊ	ㅊ	ㅊ	ㅊ	ㅊ	ㅅ	ㅍ	ㅊ	ㄴ	ㅅ	ㄴ	ㅍ
ㅅ	ㅌ	ㅊ	ㅋ	ㄹ	ㅌ	ㅊ	ㅈ	ㅎ	ㅊ	ㄱ	ㅌ	ㄱ	ㅎ
ㄷ	ㅇ	ㅊ	ㄱ	ㅅ	ㅁ	ㅊ	ㄷ	ㄴ	ㅊ	ㅇ	ㄴ	ㅂ	ㄴ
ㅎ	ㄷ	ㅈ	ㅅ	ㅇ	ㄷ	ㄹ	ㅅ	ㅎ	ㅊ	ㅍ	ㅂ	ㄹ	ㅎ

Let's Make a Sound!

Color the consonant and trace the letters.

Match Words with Pictures

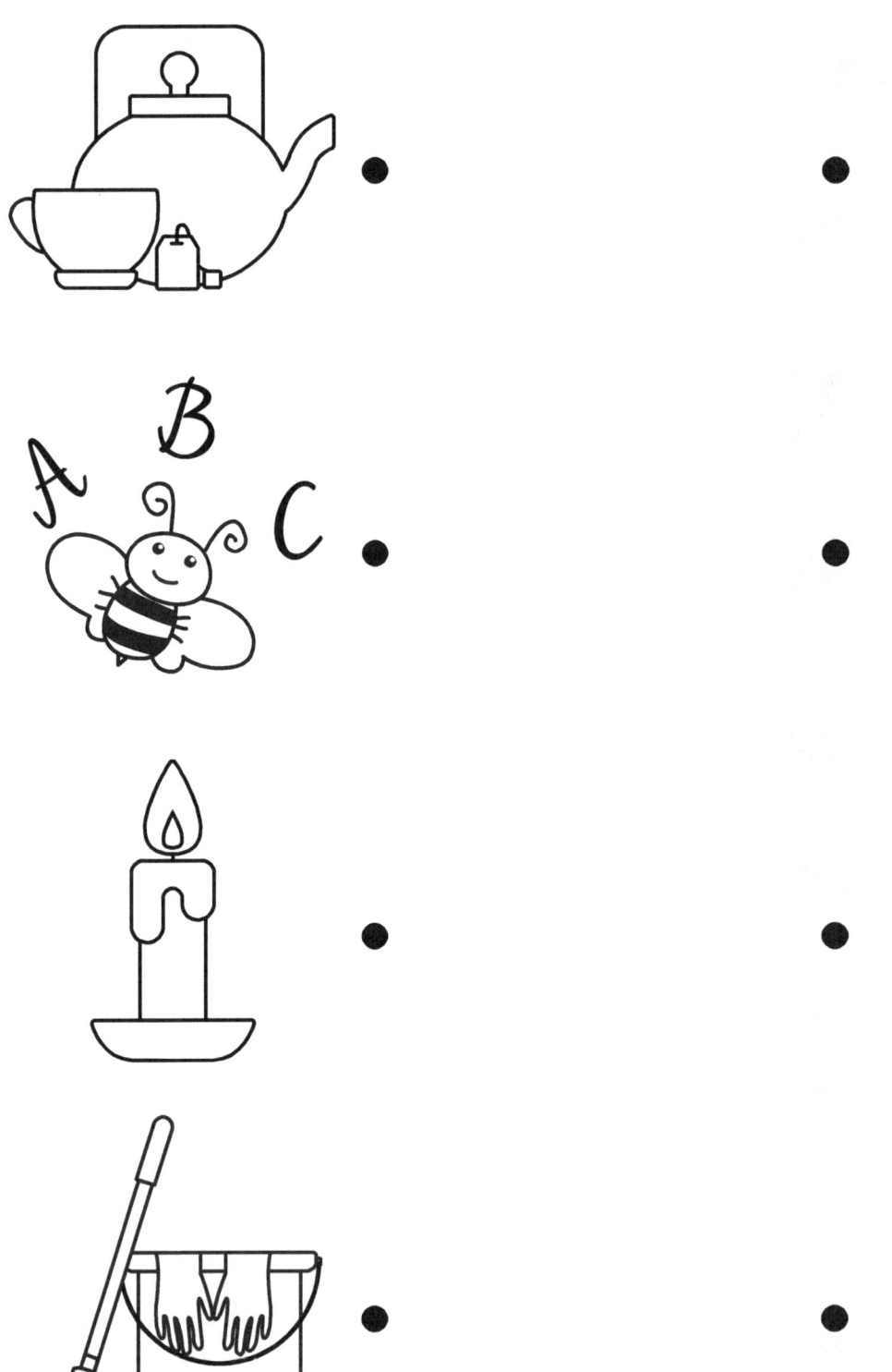

청소
[cheong-so]
Cleaning

차
[cha]
Tea

초
[cho]
Candle

철자
[cheol-ja]
Spelling

Color By the Letters

책

[chaek]

Book

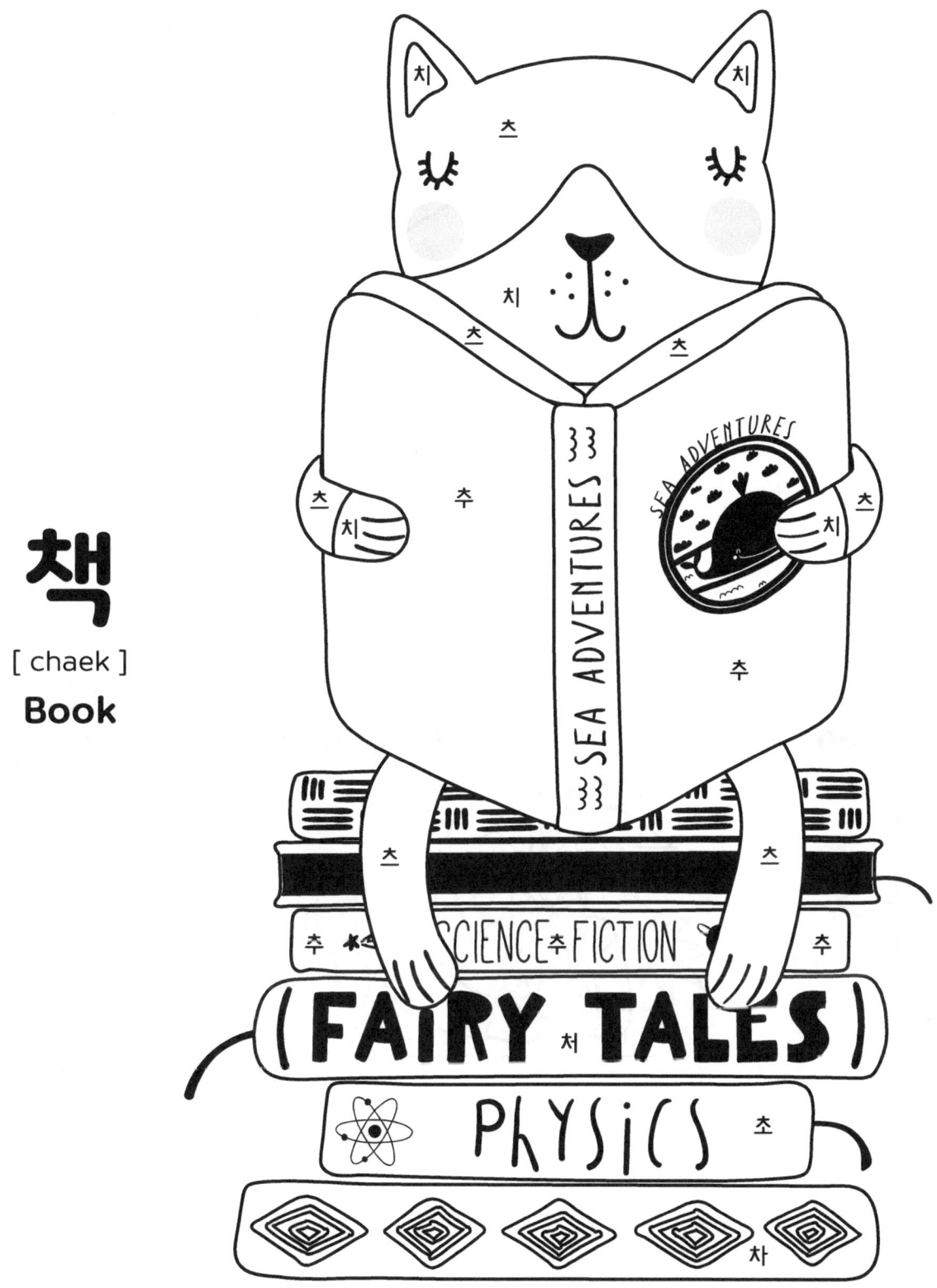

차: 초록색 (Green) **처:** 노란색 (Yellow) **초:** 보라색 (Purple)

추: 파란색 (Blue) **츠:** 회색 (Gray) **치:** 분홍색 (Pink)

Cut & Paste

Cut and paste the matching words and write it below. Find letter pieces from Pg133.

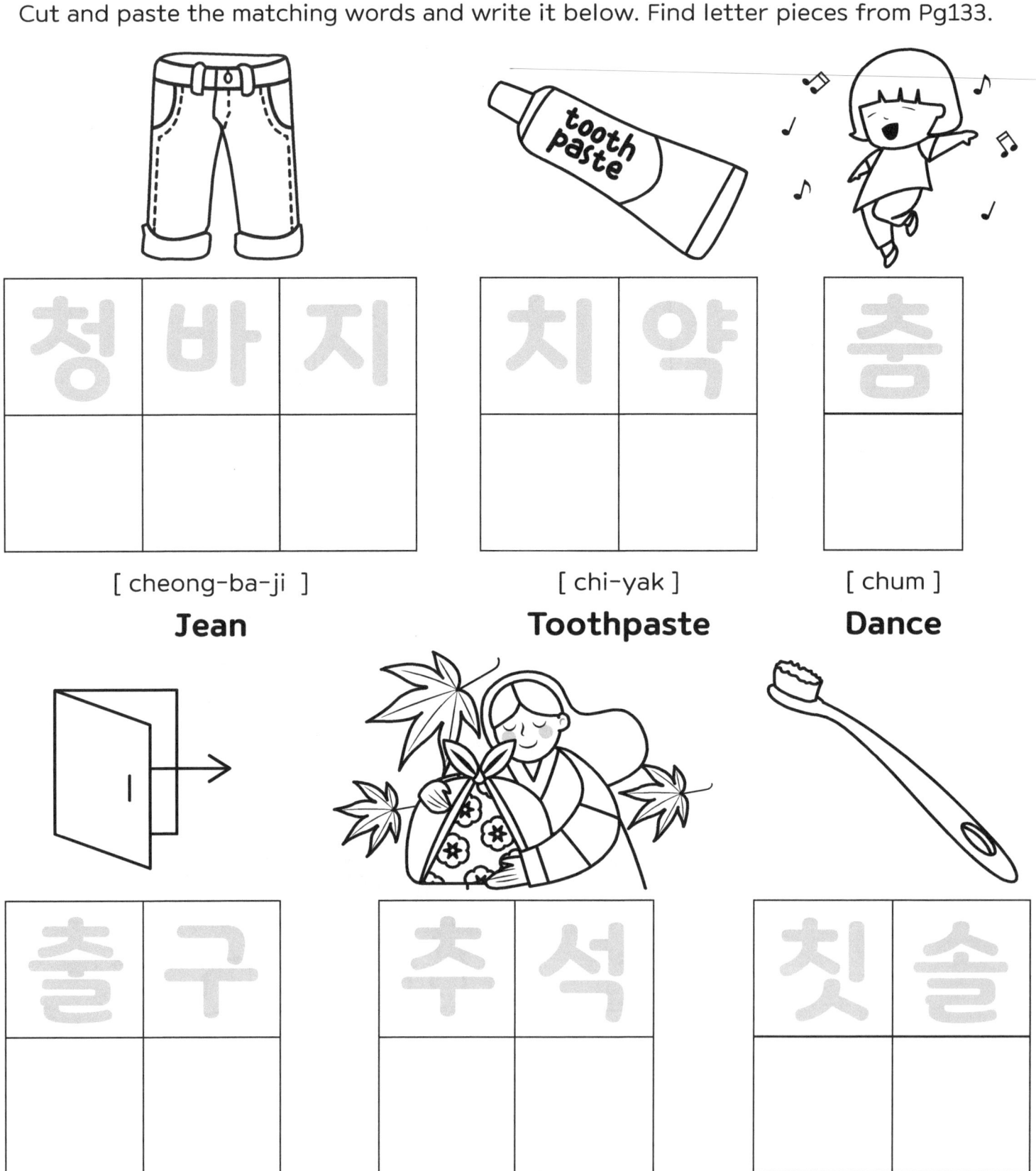

청바지

[cheong-ba-ji]

Jean

치약

[chi-yak]

Toothpaste

춤

[chum]

Dance

출구

[chul-gu]

Exit

추석

[chu-seok]

Chu-Seok

(Korean Thanksgiving)

칫솔

[chit-sol]

Toothbrush

Vocabulary Builder

운동/스포츠 | *Sports*

Cut and paste the matching words. Find letter pieces from page 133.

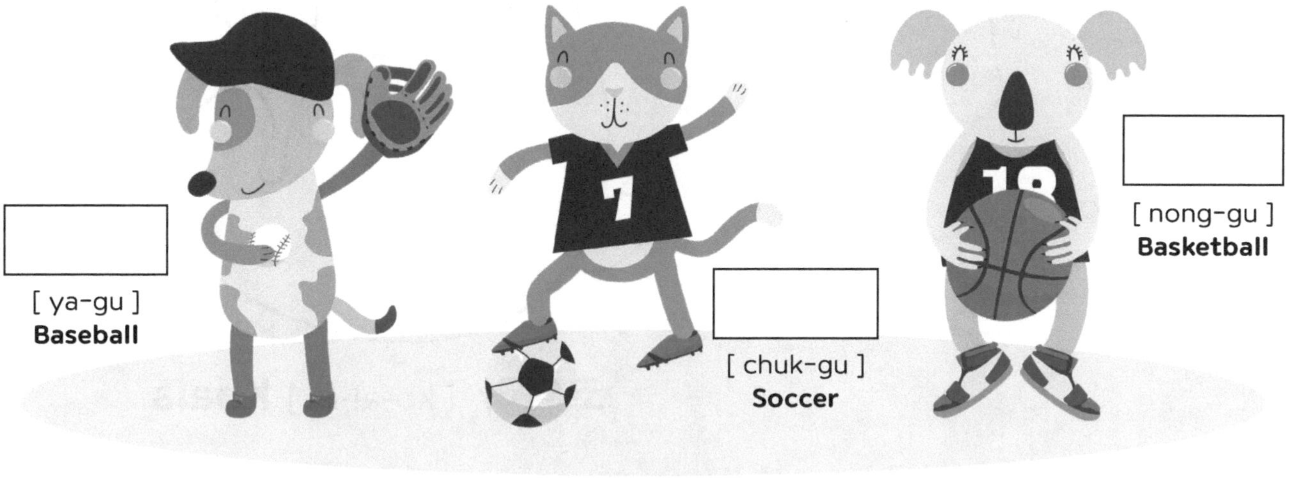
[ya-gu]
Baseball
[chuk-gu]
Soccer
[nong-gu]
Basketball

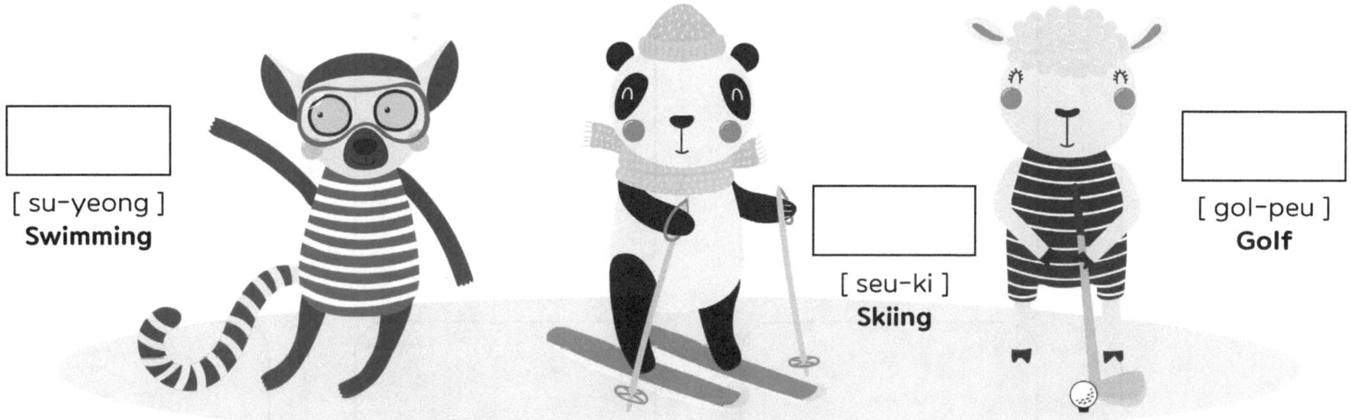
[su-yeong]
Swimming
[seu-ki]
Skiing
[gol-peu]
Golf

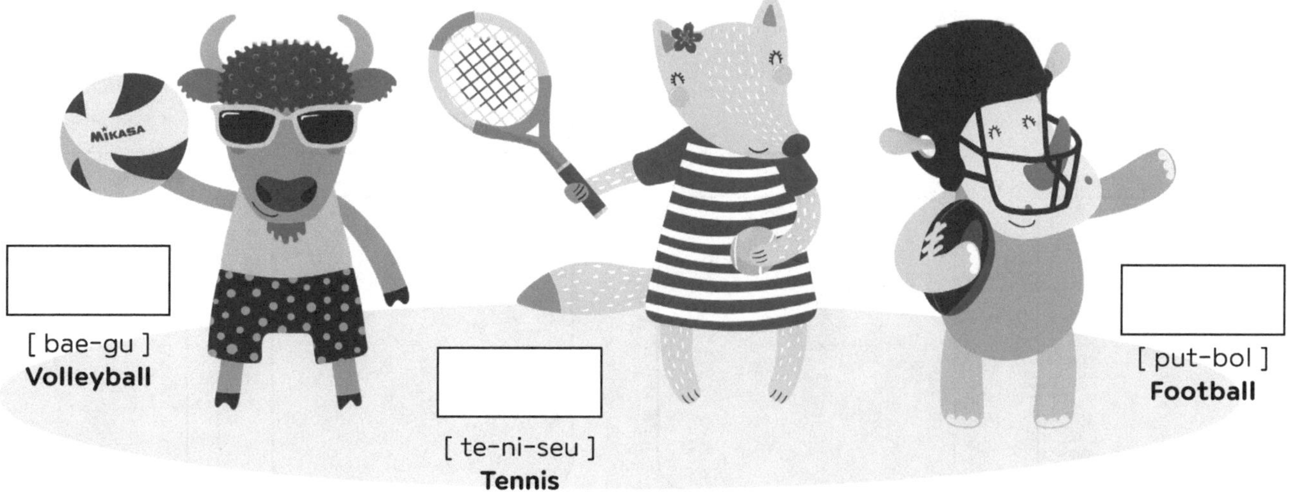
MIKASA
[bae-gu]
Volleyball
[te-ni-seu]
Tennis
[put-bol]
Football

Basic Consonant

키읔 [ki-euk]

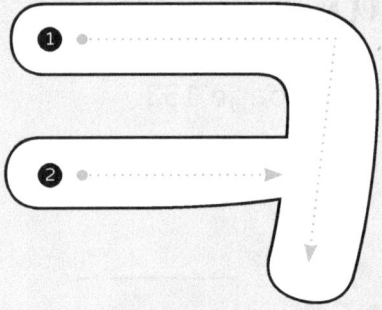

ROMANIZATION

[k]

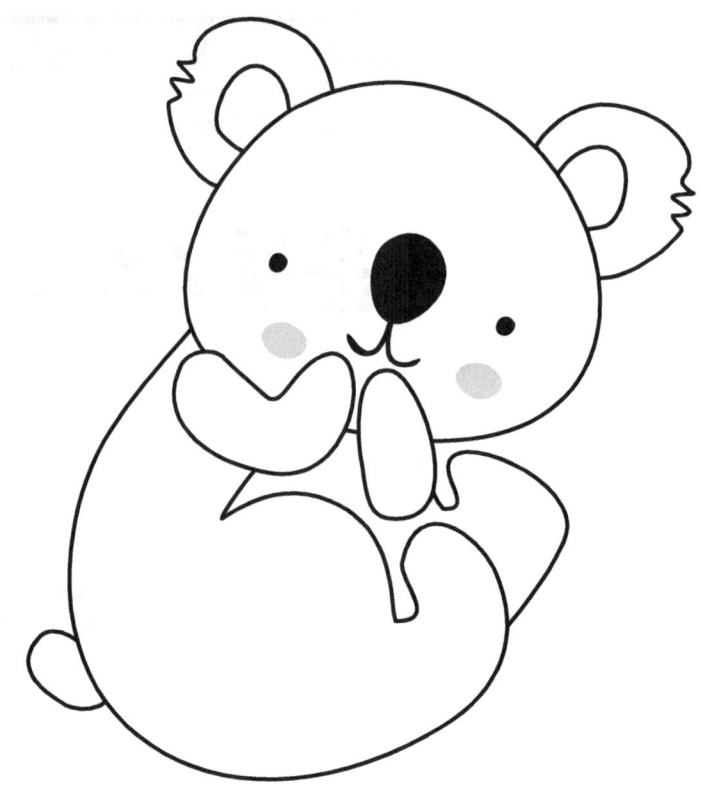

코알라 [ko-al-ra] **Koala**

Color

[ko]

Nose

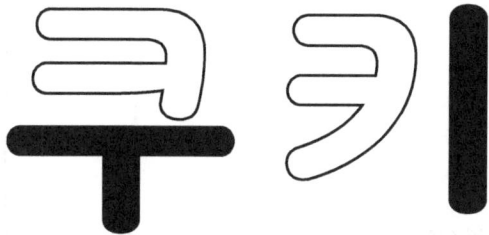

[ku-ki]

Cookie

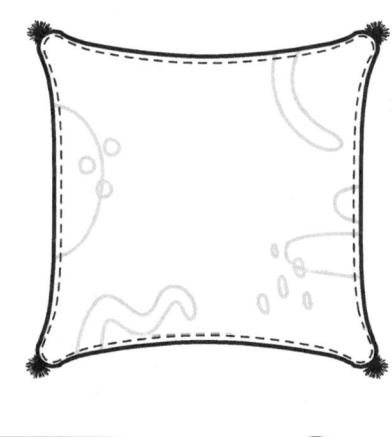

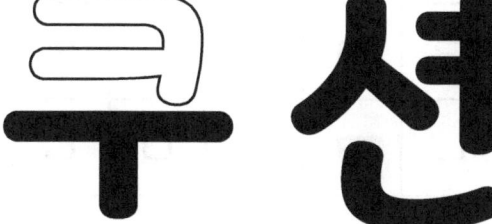

[ku-syeon]

Cushion

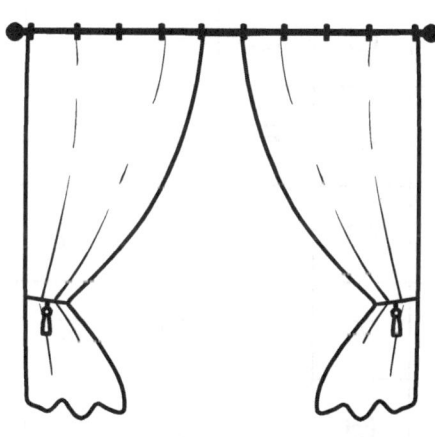

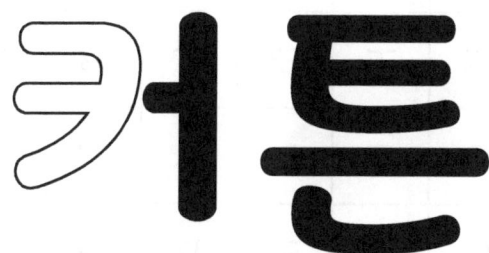

[keo-teun]

Curtains

Find and Color

[keop]

Cup

ㄹ	ㅂ	ㄴ	ㅋ	ㅋ	ㅋ	ㅋ	ㅈ	ㄴ	ㅁ	ㅋ	ㅈ	ㄷ	ㅎ
ㄴ	ㄷ	ㄹ	ㅍ	ㄹ	ㅊ	ㅋ	ㅇ	ㅋ	ㅋ	ㅋ	ㅋ	ㅂ	ㄱ	ㅊ
ㅍ	ㅁ	ㄴ	ㅋ	ㅋ	ㅋ	ㅋ	ㅂ	ㅌ	ㄷ	ㅋ	ㅈ	ㄷ	ㅁ
ㄴ	ㅋ	ㄹ	ㅍ	ㅈ	ㅊ	ㅋ	ㅈ	ㅅ	ㄹ	ㅋ	ㅂ	ㅁ	ㅊ
ㅊ	ㅂ	ㄴ	ㅅ	ㅋ	ㅍ	ㅈ	ㅂ	ㅇ	ㅋ	ㅅ	ㄱ	ㄷ	ㅅ
ㅈ	ㅈ	ㄹ	ㅍ	ㅋ	ㅋ	ㅋ	ㅋ	ㅋ	ㅋ	ㄴ	ㄹ	ㅌ	ㅊ
ㅇ	ㅁ	ㄴ	ㅅ	ㅋ	ㅌ	ㅊ	ㅂ	ㄴ	ㅋ	ㅅ	ㅁ	ㄷ	ㅈ
ㄴ	ㅈ	ㄹ	ㅍ	ㅋ	ㅋ	ㅋ	ㅋ	ㅋ	ㅋ	ㅋ	ㅍ	ㅇ	ㅌ	ㅊ

Let's Make a Sound!

Color the consonant and trace the letters.

Match Words with Pictures

콩
[kong]
Bean

커피
[keo-pi]
Coffee

코리아
[ko-ri-a]
Korea (한국)

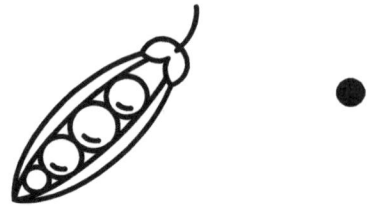

코코아
[ko-ko-a]
Cocoa

Color By the Letters

카우보이

[ka-u-bo-i]

Cowboy

카: 보라색 (Purple) **커:** 노란색 (Yellow) **켜:** 검정색 (Black) **코:** 빨간색 (Red)

쿠: 파란색 (Blue) **큐:** 갈색 (Blue) **크:** 회색 (Gray) **키:** 분홍색 (Pink)

Cut & Paste

Cut and paste the matching words and write it below. Find letter pieces from page 135.

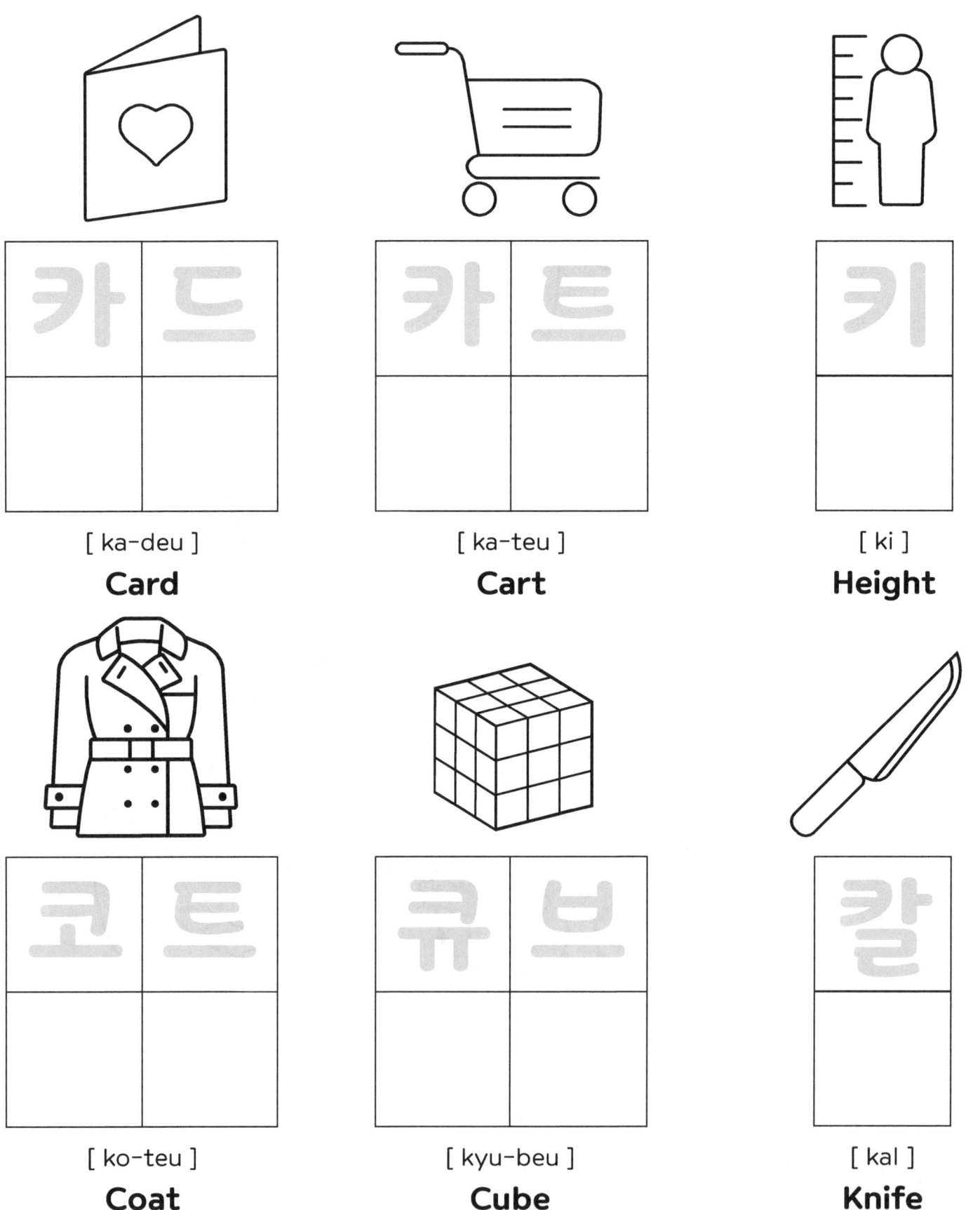

[ka-deu]
Card

[ka-teu]
Cart

[ki]
Height

[ko-teu]
Coat

[kyu-beu]
Cube

[kal]
Knife

Vocabulary Builder

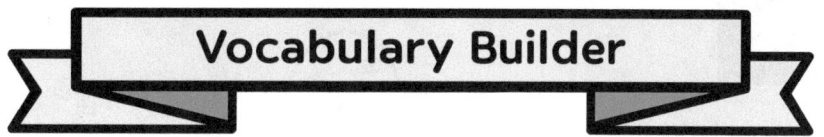

교통 수단 | Transportation

Cut and paste the matching words. Find letter pieces from page 135.

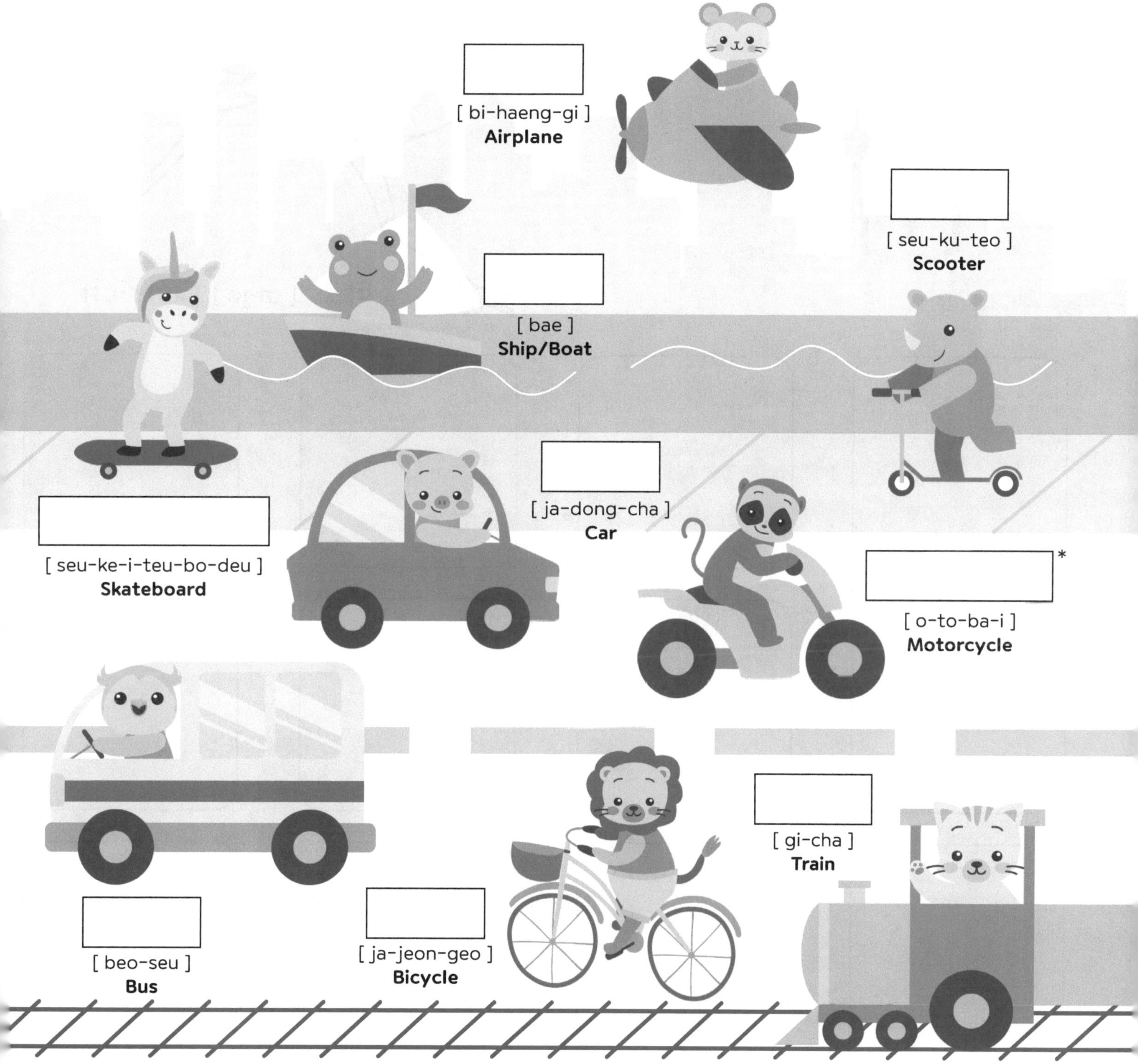
[bi-haeng-gi]
Airplane
[seu-ku-teo]
Scooter
[bae]
Ship/Boat
[ja-dong-cha]
Car
[seu-ke-i-teu-bo-deu]
Skateboard
*
[o-to-ba-i]
Motorcycle
[gi-cha]
Train
[beo-seu]
Bus
[ja-jeon-geo]
Bicycle

*오토바이 is originated from a localized Japanese-English word, automatic bicycle.

티읕 [ti-eut]

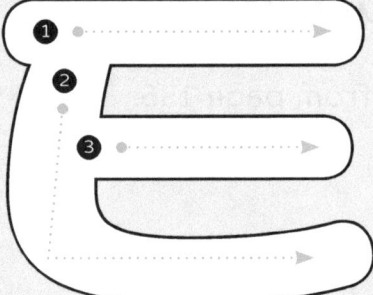

ROMANIZATION

[t]

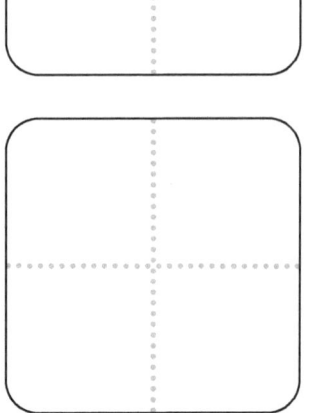

타조 [ta-jo] **Ostrich**

Color

트럭
[teu-reok]
Truck

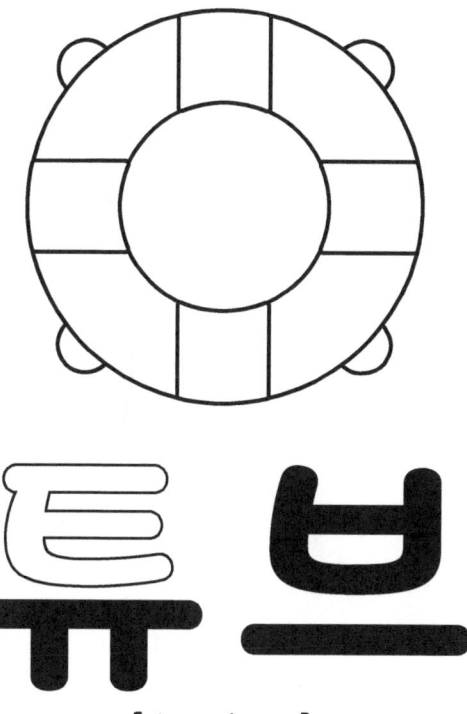

튜브
[tyu-beu]
Tube

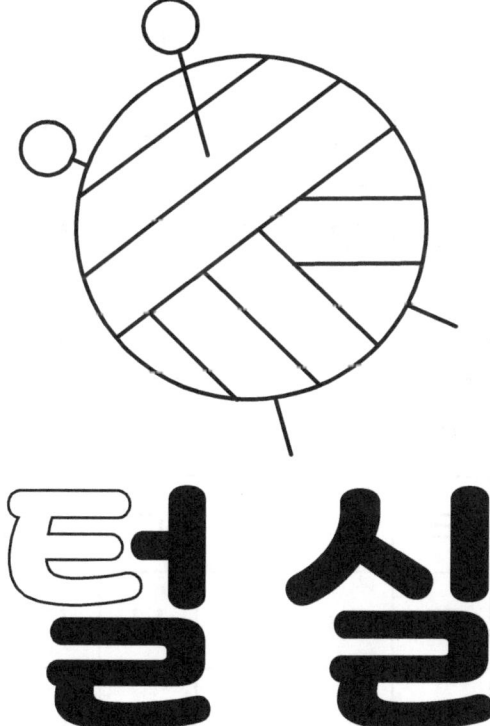

털실
[teol-sil]
Yarn

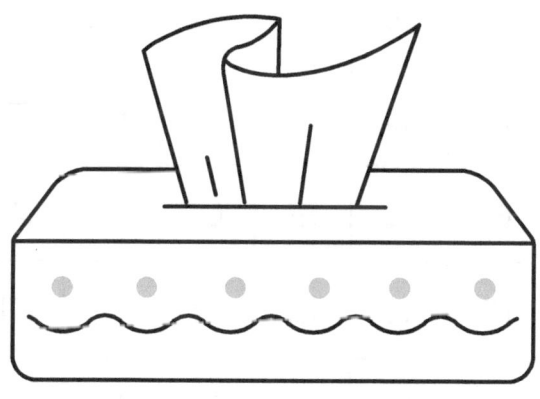

티슈
[ti-syu]
Tissue

Find and Color ㅌ

[to-ma-to]

Tomato

ㅌ	ㅌ	ㅌ	ㅂ	ㄴ	ㅅ	ㅎ	ㅂ	ㄴ	ㄷ	ㄴ	ㅌ	ㅌ	ㅌ
ㅌ	ㅇ	ㅅ	ㄱ	ㅌ	ㅌ	ㅌ	ㅅ	ㅌ	ㄱ	ㅊ	ㅌ	ㅇ	ㅅ
ㅌ	ㅌ	ㅌ	ㄴ	ㅌ	ㅅ	ㅌ	ㅊ	ㅌ	ㄹ	ㅍ	ㅌ	ㅌ	ㅌ
ㅌ	ㄴ	ㅂ	ㄹ	ㅌ	ㄱ	ㅌ	ㅍ	ㅌ	ㅇ	ㅇ	ㅌ	ㄴ	ㅂ
ㅌ	ㅌ	ㅌ	ㄱ	ㅌ	ㄹ	ㅌ	ㅊ	ㅌ	ㅌ	ㄱ	ㅌ	ㅌ	ㅌ
ㄷ	ㅇ	ㅈ	ㅅ	ㅌ	ㅌ	ㅌ	ㄷ	ㅌ	ㄷ	ㅊ	ㄷ	ㅇ	ㅈ
ㅂ	ㅌ	ㅊ	ㄹ	ㄹ	ㄹ	ㅅ	ㅊ	ㅌ	ㅂ	ㄱ	ㅂ	ㅌ	ㅊ
ㅌ	ㅌ	ㅌ	ㅌ	ㅇ	ㅊ	ㅅ	ㅇ	ㄷ	ㅌ	ㅅ	ㅍ	ㅌ	ㅌ	ㅌ

Let's Make a Sound!

Color the consonant and trace the letters.

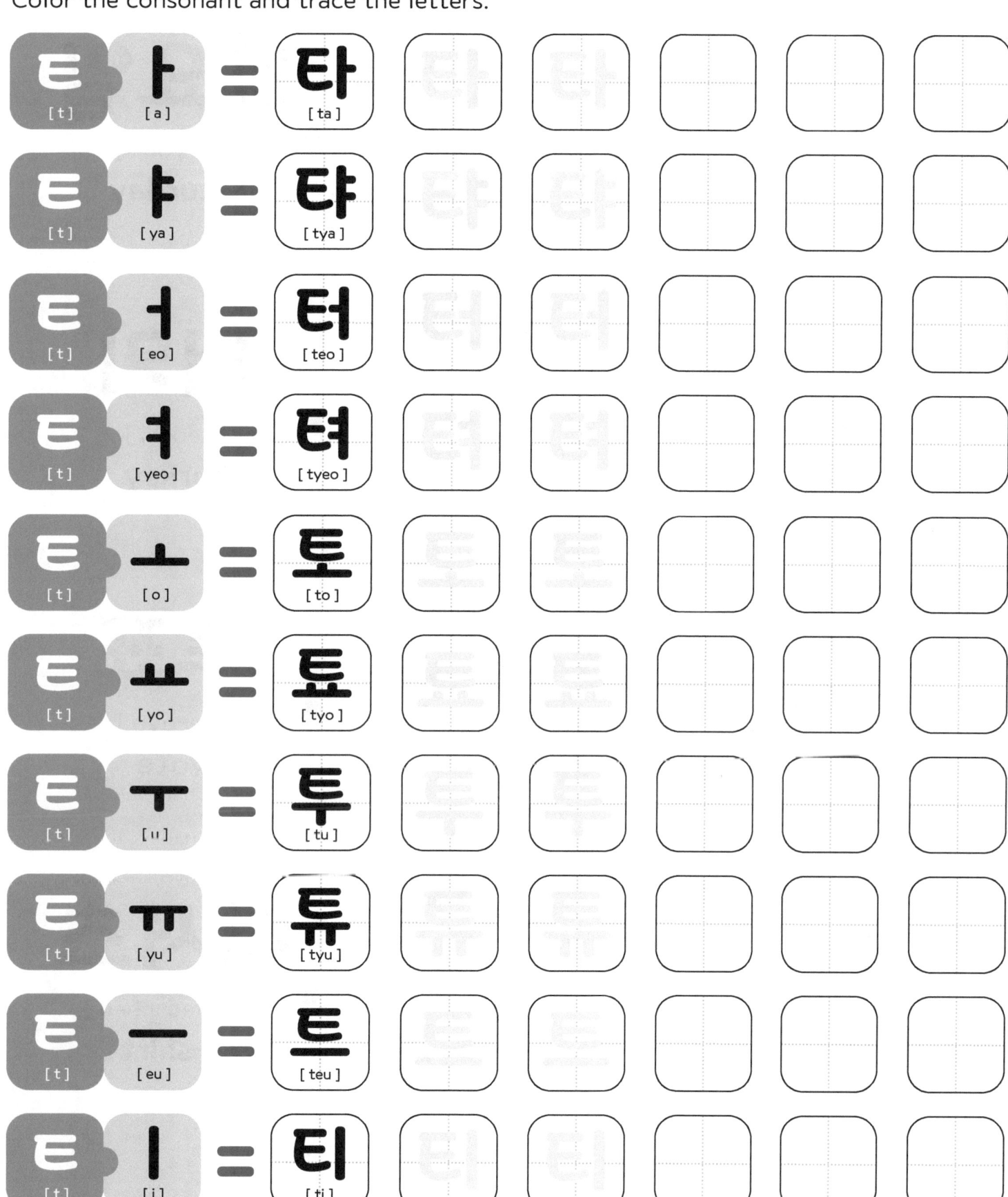

Match Words with Pictures

토요일
[to-yo-il]
Saturday

터키
[teo-ki]
Turkey

투표
[tu-pyo]
Vote

Sat

티셔츠
[ti-syeo-cheu]
T-shirt

Color By the Letters

투투

[tu-tu]

Tutu

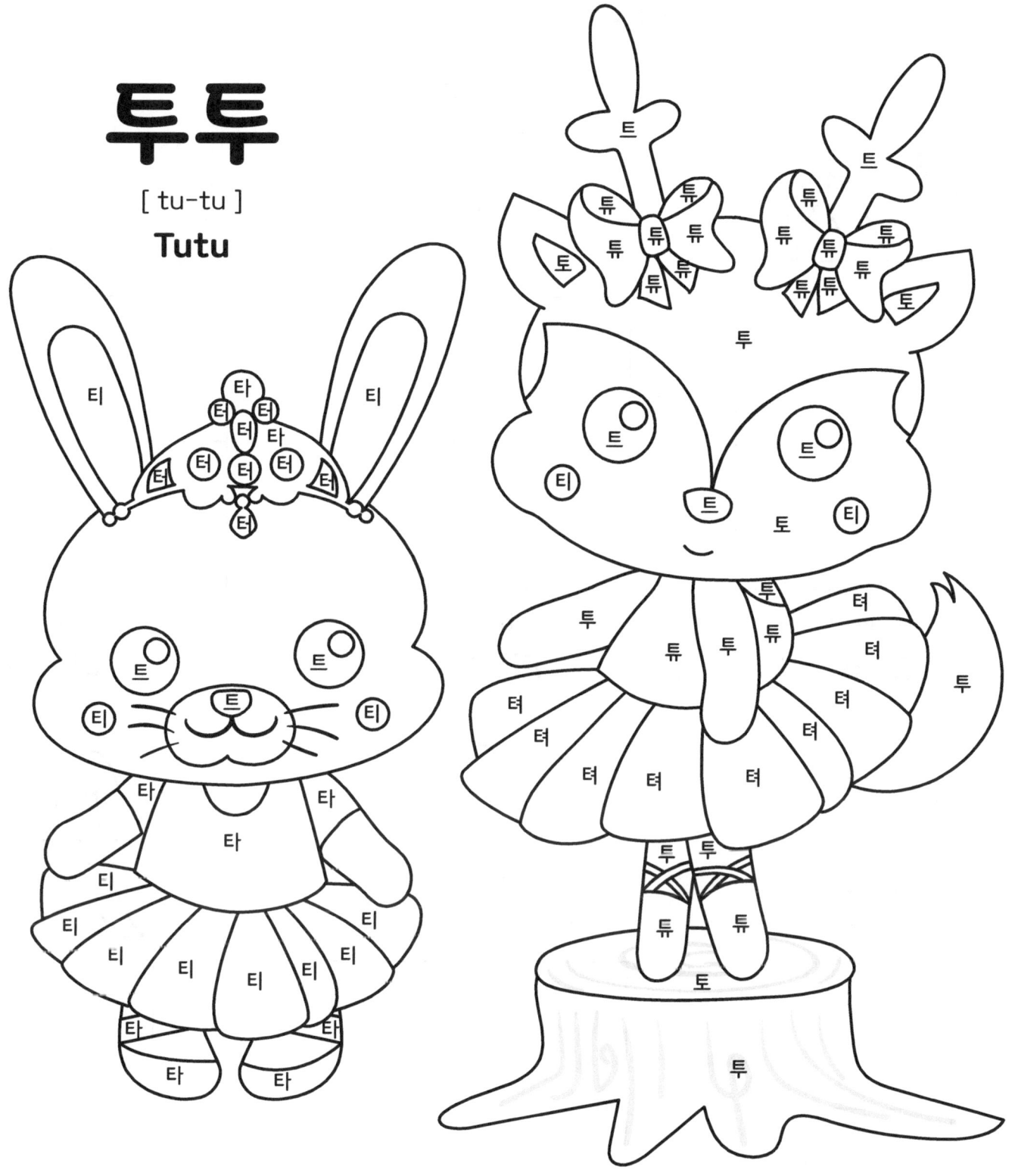

타: 보라색 (Purple)　**터:** 노란색 (Yellow)　**텨:** 하늘색 (Light Blue)

토: 살구색 (Apricot)　**투:** 갈색 (Brown)　**튜:** 연두색 (Lime Green)

트: 검정색 (Black)　**티:** 분홍색 (Pink)

Cut & Paste

Cut and paste the matching words and write it below. Find letter pieces from page 135.

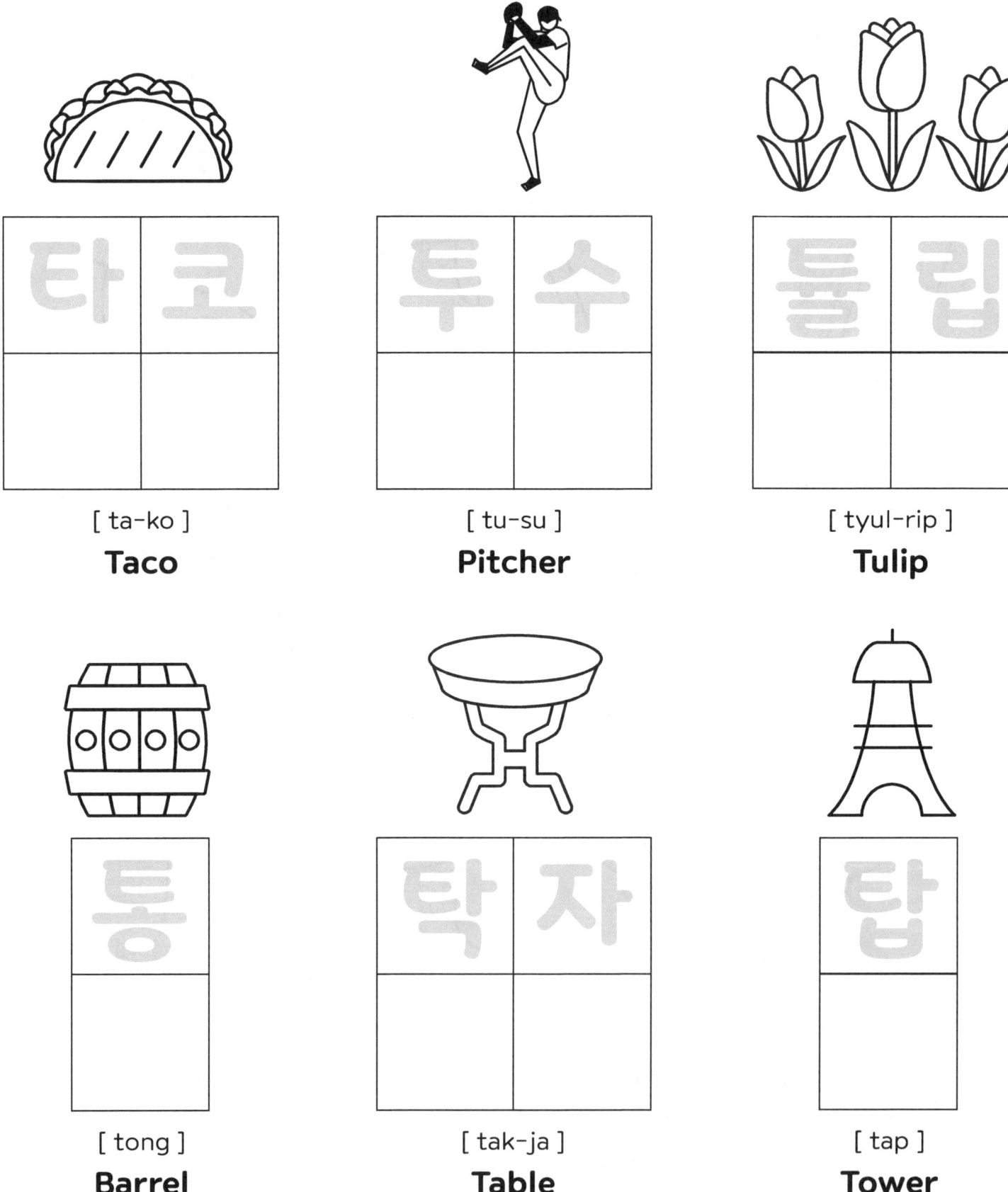

[ta-ko]
Taco

[tu-su]
Pitcher

[tyul-rip]
Tulip

[tong]
Barrel

[tak-ja]
Table

[tap]
Tower

반댓말 | Opposites

Cut and paste the matching words. Find letter pieces from page 135.

[gil-da]
Tall

[jjal-da]
Short

[keu-da]
Big

[jak-da]
Small

[man-ta]
More

[jeok-da]
Less

[ap]
Front

[oen-jjok]
Left

[o-reun-jjok]
Right

[dwi]
Back

피읖 [pi-eup]

ROMANIZATION

[p]

표범
[pyo-beom]
Leopard

Color

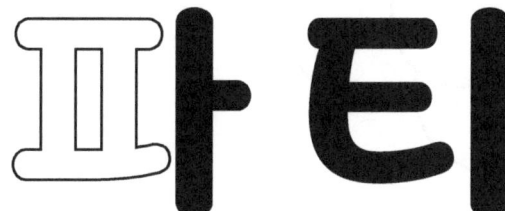

[pa-ti]
Party

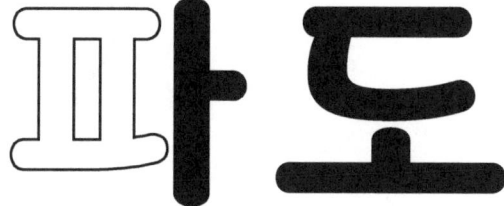

[pa-do]
Wave

[peo-jeul]
Puzzle

[pi-ja]
Pizza

Find and Color ㅍ

[po-do]

Grapes

ㄹ	ㅂ	ㄴ	ㅂ	ㄴ	ㅅ	ㅎ	ㅂ	ㄴ	ㄷ	ㄴ	ㄴ	ㅂ	ㄱ	ㄹ
ㅊ	ㅍ	ㅍ	ㅍ	ㅍ	ㅍ	ㅊ	ㅅ	ㅍ	ㅍ	ㅍ	ㅍ	ㅍ	ㅍ	ㅇ
ㅂ	ㅇ	ㅍ	ㄱ	ㅍ	ㅂ	ㅅ	ㅊ	ㅍ	ㄹ	ㄷ	ㅂ	ㄱ	ㅂ
ㅊ	ㅂ	ㅍ	ㄹ	ㅍ	ㄱ	ㄷ	ㄷ	ㅍ	ㅇ	ㅈ	ㅅ	ㄴ	ㄷ
ㅅ	ㅍ	ㅍ	ㅍ	ㅍ	ㅍ	ㅊ	ㅊ	ㅍ	ㅍ	ㅍ	ㅍ	ㅍ	ㅎ
ㄷ	ㅇ	ㅇ	ㄱ	ㄷ	ㄱ	ㅇ	ㄷ	ㄹ	ㄷ	ㄱ	ㄴ	ㅂ	ㄴ
ㅂ	ㅅ	ㅊ	ㅍ	ㄹ	ㅋ	ㅅ	ㅊ	ㅂ	ㅊ	ㅍ	ㄹ	ㅎ	ㅂ
ㅎ	ㅍ	ㅍ	ㅍ	ㅍ	ㅍ	ㅇ	ㄷ	ㅍ	ㅍ	ㅍ	ㅍ	ㅍ	ㅎ

Let's Make a Sound!

Color the consonant and trace the letters.

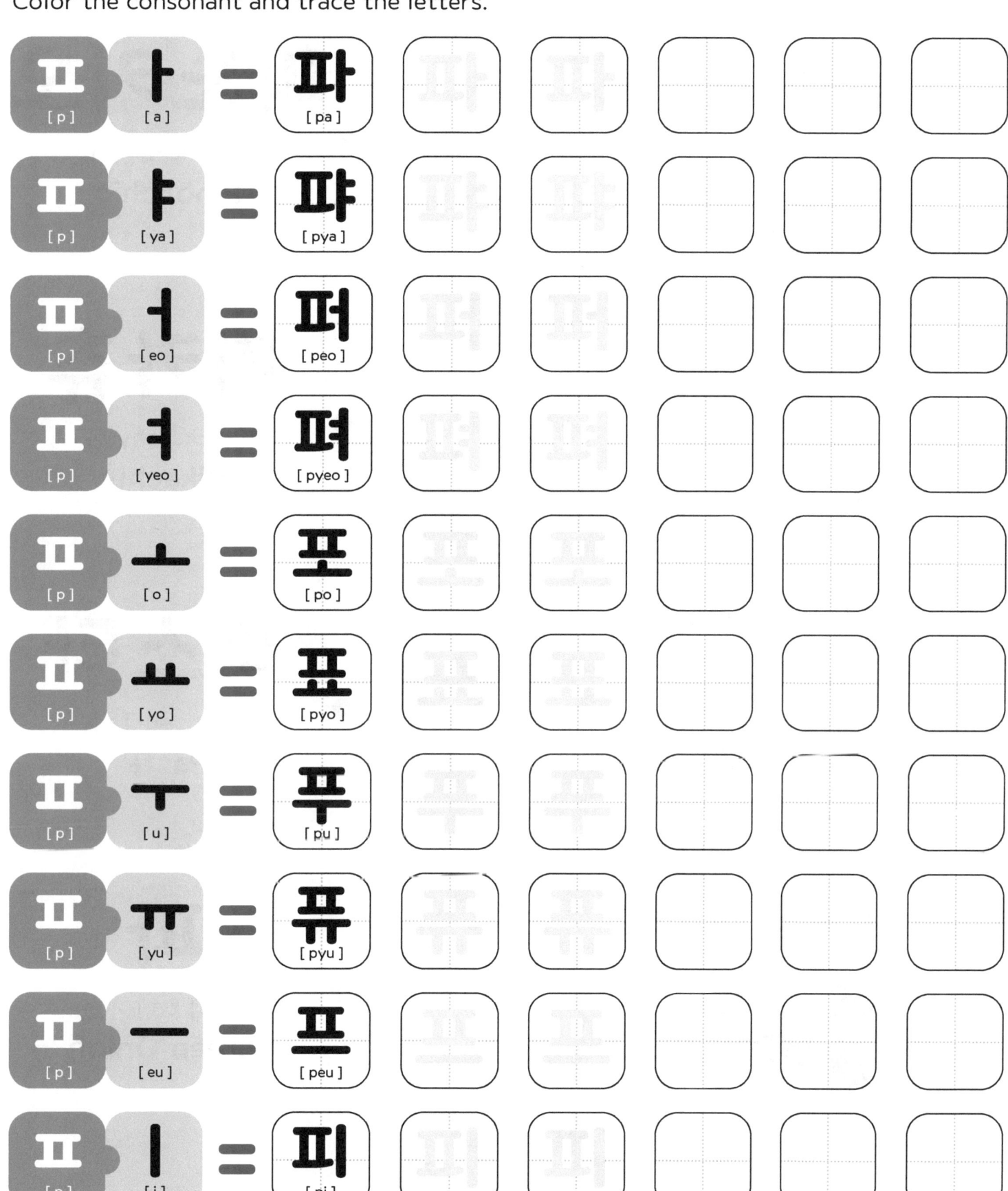

Match Words with Pictures

[pi-no-ki-o]
Pinocchio

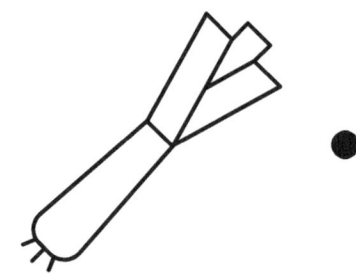

[pi-ka-chyu]
Pikachu

파스타
[pa-seu-ta]
Pasta

[pa]
Green Onion

Color By the Letters

파티

[pa-ti]

Party

파: 주황색 (Orange)　**퍼:** 노란색 (Yellow)　**펴:** 살구색 (Apricot)　**포:** 빨간색 (Red)

표: 파란색 (Blue)　**푸:** 초록색 (Green)　**프:** 갈색 (Brown)　**피:** 분홍색 (Pink)

Cut & Paste

Cut and paste the matching words and write it below. Find letter pieces from page 137.

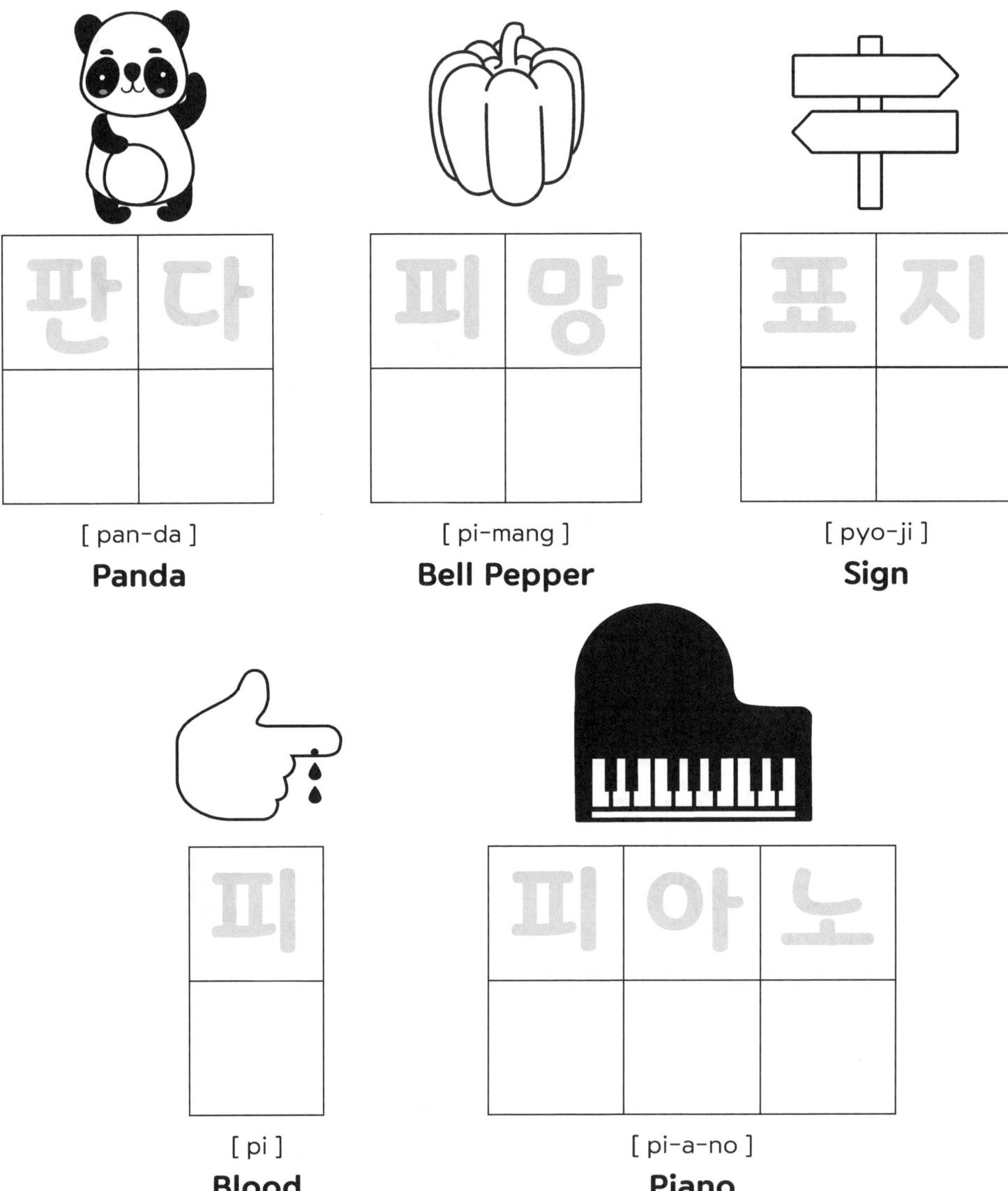

[pan-da]
Panda

[pi-mang]
Bell Pepper

[pyo-ji]
Sign

[pi]
Blood

[pi-a-no]
Piano

나라/국가 | Conturies

Cut and paste the matching words. Find letter pieces from page 137.

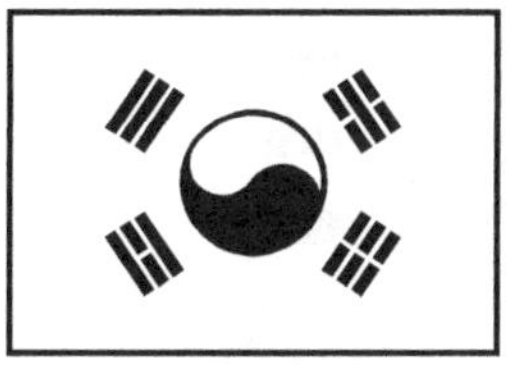

[han-guk]
Korea

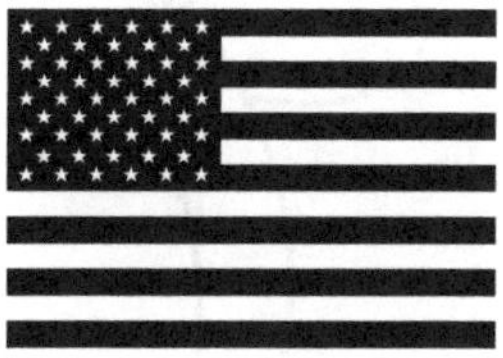

[mi-guk]
USA

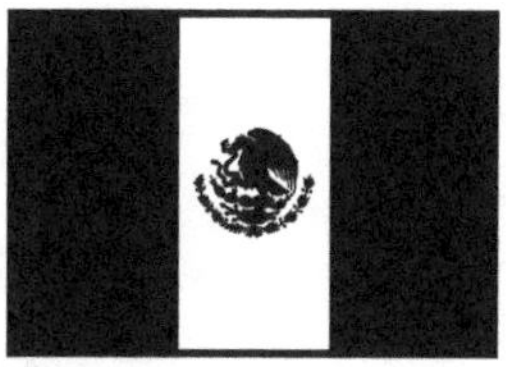

[mek-si-ko]
Mexico

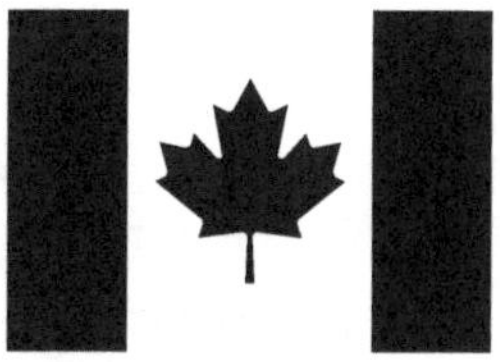

[kae-na-da]
Canada

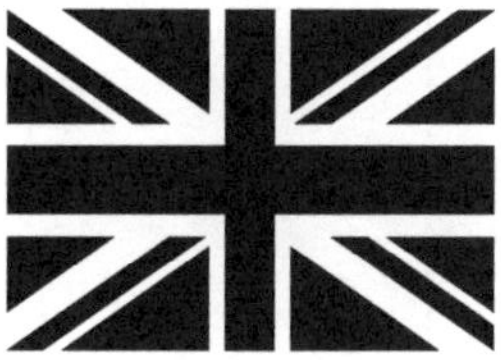

[yeong-guk]
Great Britain

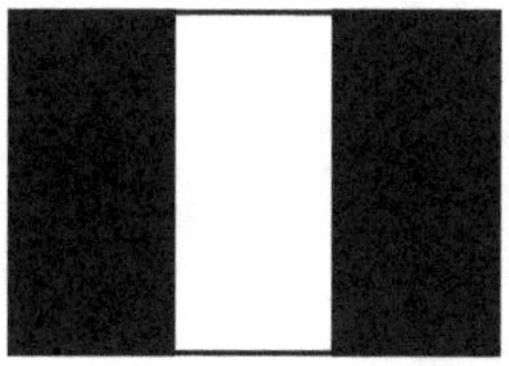

[peu-rang-seu]
France

[dok-il]
Germany

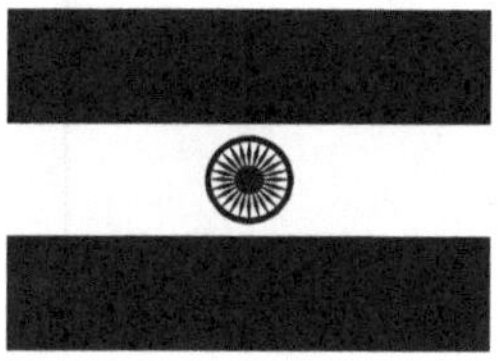

[in-do]
India

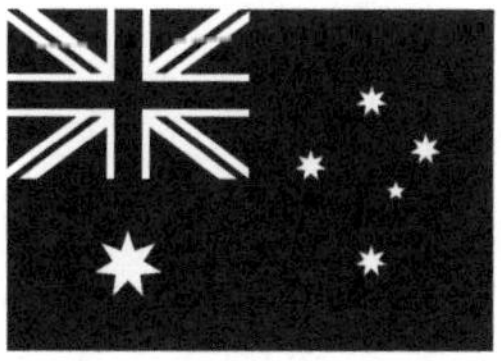

[ho-ju]
Australia

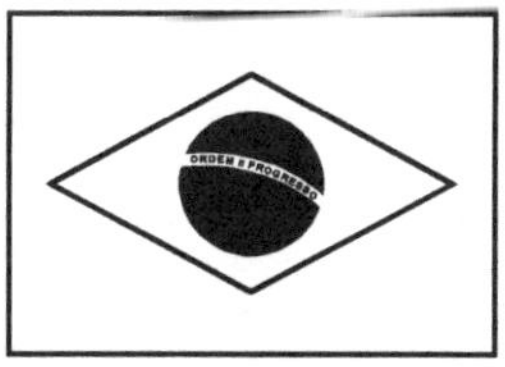

[beu-ra-jil]
Brazil

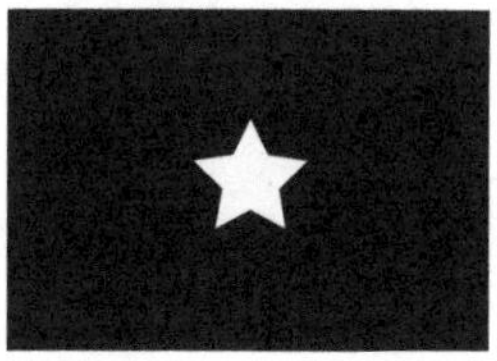

[be-teu-nam]
Vietnam

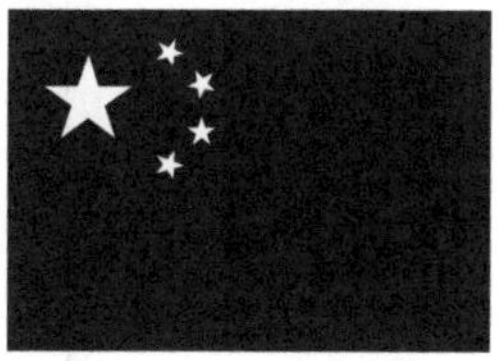

[jung-guk]
China

히읗 [hi-eut]

ROMANIZATION

[h]

호랑이
[ho-rang-i]
Tiger

Color

형

[hyeong]

Older Brother*

*A younger male to call an older male or sibling

1

하나

[ha-na]

One

후추

[hu-chu]

Pepper

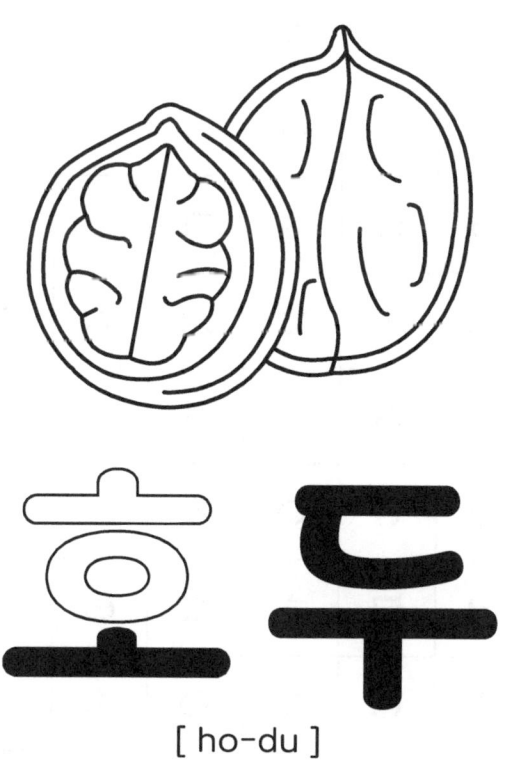

호두

[ho-du]

Walnut

Find and Color

[ha-ma]

Hippopotamus

ㄹ	ㅅ	ㅎ	ㅂ	ㄴ	ㅅ	ㅈ	ㅂ	ㄴ	ㄷ	ㄴ	ㅂ	ㅍ	ㅂ
ㄴ	ㅎ	ㅎ	ㅎ	ㄱ	ㅎ	ㄴ	ㅈ	ㄱ	ㅍ	ㅌ	ㅊ	ㅎ	ㅇ
ㅂ	ㅇ	ㅅ	ㄱ	ㄹ	ㅎ	ㄹ	ㅌ	ㅎ	ㅎ	ㅎ	ㅎ	ㅂ	ㅎ
ㅊ	ㅅ	ㅎ	ㅅ	ㅅ	ㅎ	ㅈ	ㄹ	ㅎ	ㅇ	ㅎ	ㅅ	ㅎ	ㅍ
ㅁ	ㅎ	ㅅ	ㅎ	ㅁ	ㅎ	ㅎ	ㅂ	ㅎ	ㄱ	ㅎ	ㄱ	ㅎ	ㅎ
ㄹ	ㅎ	ㅇ	ㅎ	ㄹ	ㅎ	ㄷ	ㄷ	ㅎ	ㅎ	ㅎ	ㄴ	ㅎ	ㄴ
ㅂ	ㄹ	ㅎ	ㅍ	ㅂ	ㅎ	ㅁ	ㅍ	ㄹ	ㅂ	ㄱ	ㅅ	ㅎ	ㅍ
ㅊ	ㄴ	ㄷ	ㄷ	ㅇ	ㅊ	ㅎ	ㄹ	ㄹ	ㄹ	ㅅ	ㅍ	ㅂ	ㅈ

Let's Make a Sound!

Color the consonant and trace the letters.

Match Words with Pictures

호박
[ho-bak]
Pumpkin

화가
[hwa-ga]
Artist

휴지통
[hyu-ji-tong]
Trash Can

한복
[han-bok]
Hanbok*

* Traditional Korean
clothes

Color By the Letters

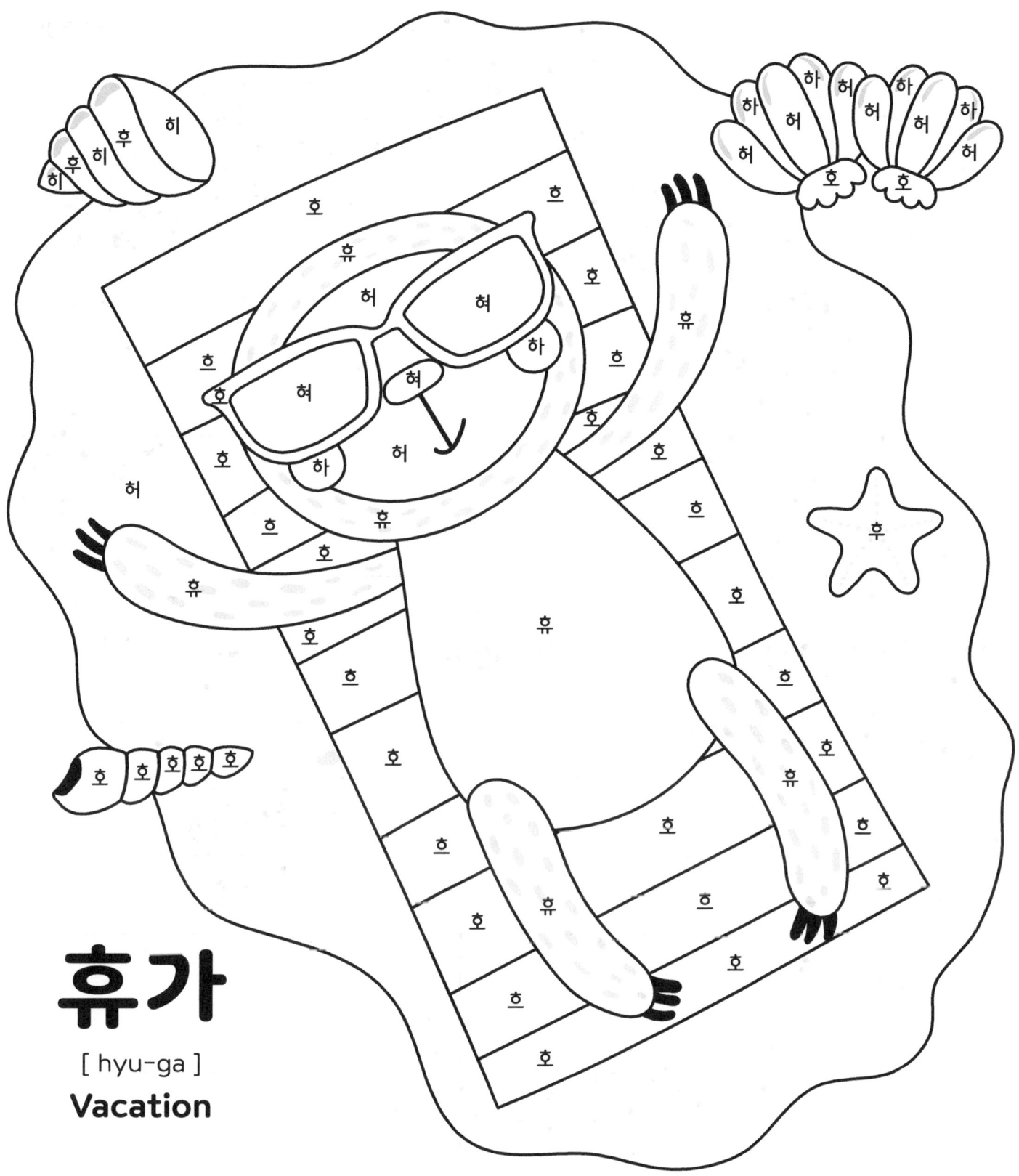

휴가

[hyu-ga]

Vacation

하: 분홍색 (Pink) **허:** 노란색 (Yellow) **혀:** 검정색 (Black) **호:** 보라색 (Purple)

후: 주황색 (Orange) **휴:** 갈색 (Brown) **흐:** 초록색 (Green) **히:** 빨간색 (Red)

Cut & Paste

Cut and paste the matching words and write it below. Find letter pieces from page 137.

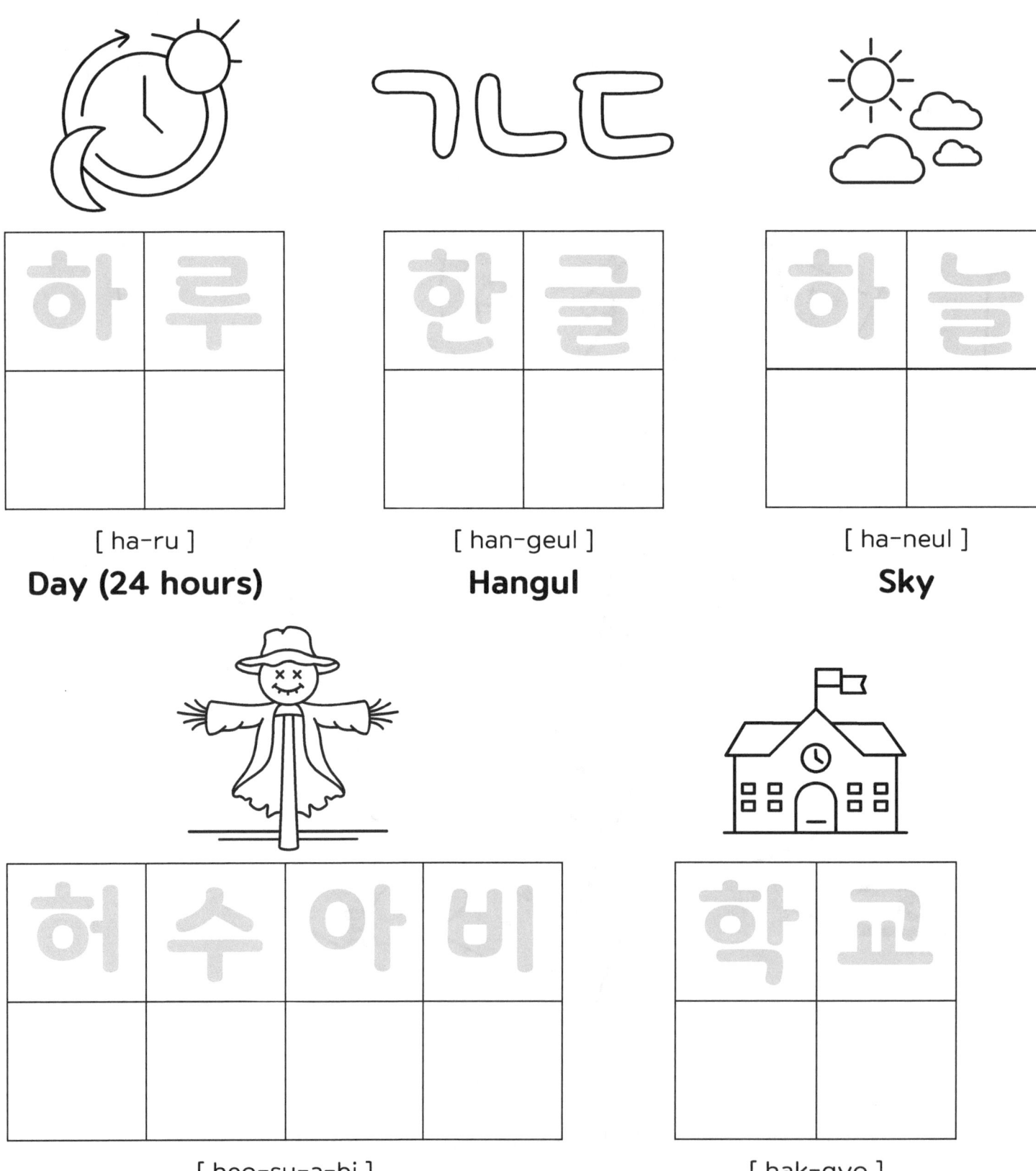

[ha-ru]
Day (24 hours)

[han-geul]
Hangul

[ha-neul]
Sky

[heo-su-a-bi]
Scarecrow

[hak-gyo]
School

Vocabulary Builder

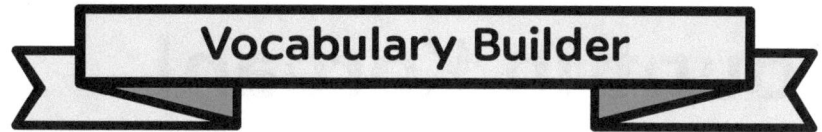

기념일 & 공휴일 | Festivals & Holidays

Cut and paste the matching words. Find letter pieces from page 137.

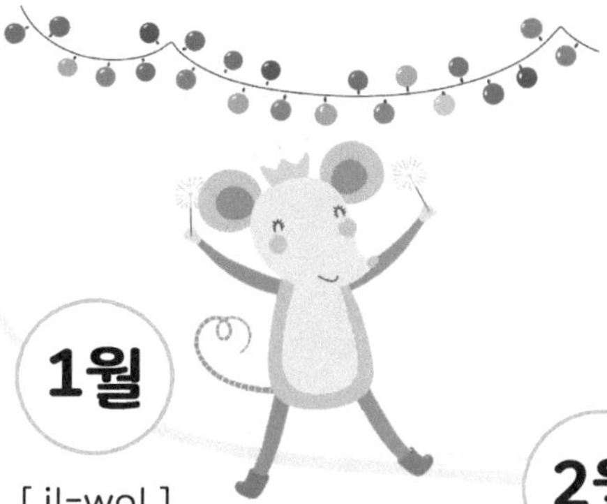

1월
[il-wol]
January

[sin-jeong]
New Year

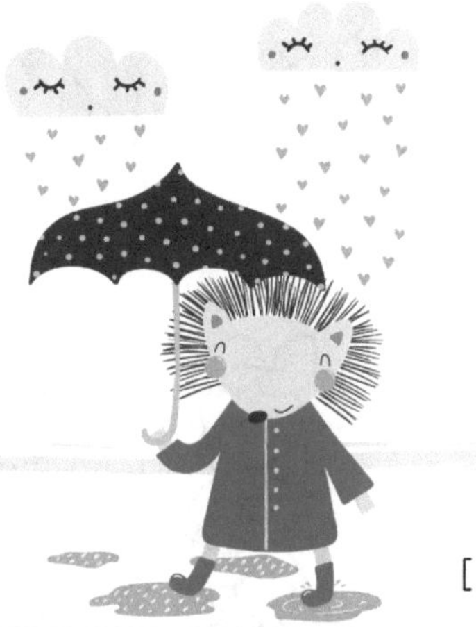

2월
[i-wol]
February

[bal-ren-ta-in-de-i]
Valentine's Day

3월
[sam-wol]
March

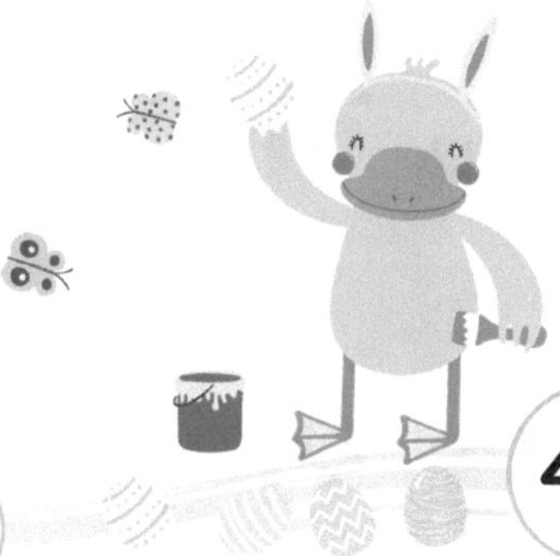

4월
[sa-wol]
April

[bu-hwal-jeol]
Easter

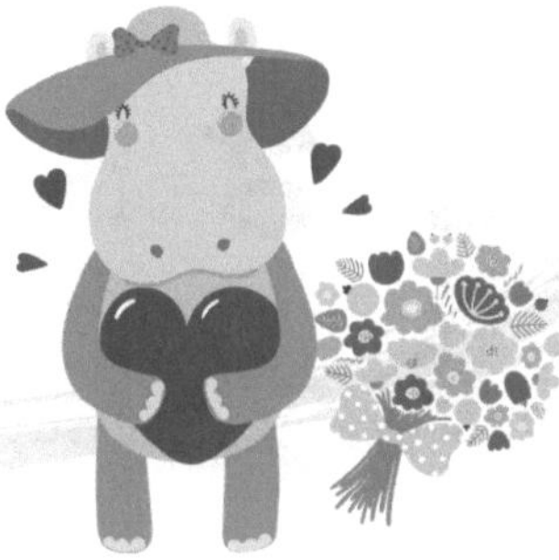

5월
[o-wol]
May

[eo-meo-ni-eu-nal]
Mother's Day

6월
[yu-wol]
June

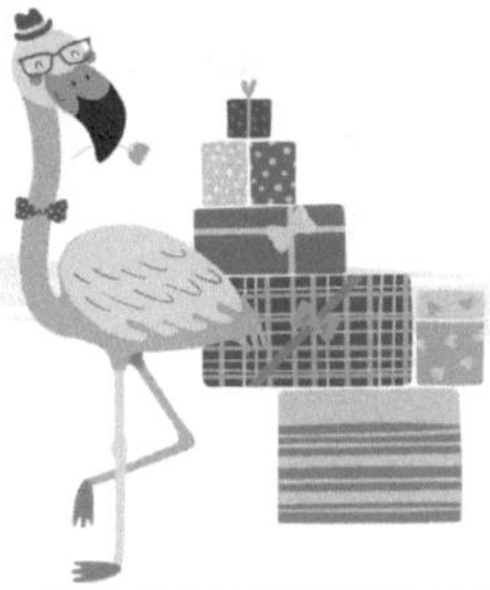

7월
[chil-wol]
July

[a-beo-ji-eu-nal]
Father's Day

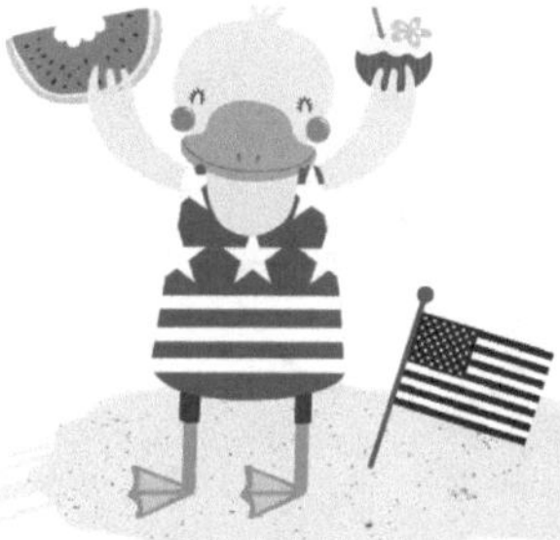

8월
[pal-wol]
August

[dok-rip-gi-nyeom-il]
Independence Day

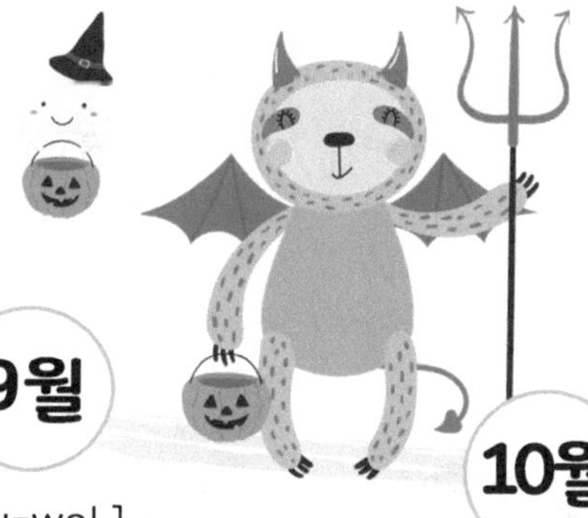

9월
[gu-wol]
September

[hal-ro-win]
Halloween

10월
[si-wol]
October

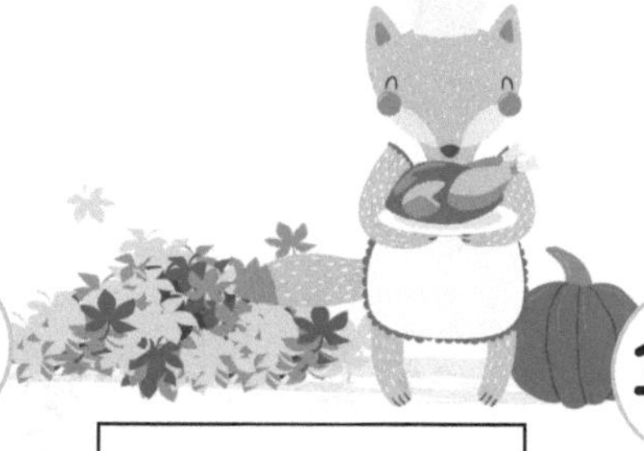

[chu-su-gam-sa-jeol]
Thanksgiving

11월
[sip-il-wol]
November

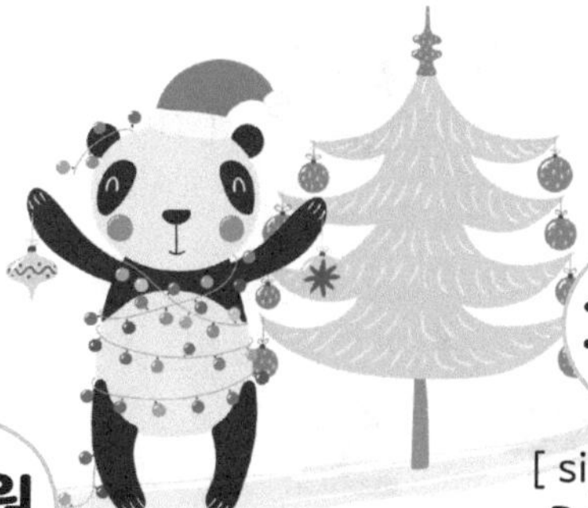

12월
[sip-i-wol]
December

[keu-ri-seu-ma-seu]
Christmas

Let's Count in Korean!

Sino Korean: 일, 이, 삼, 사, 오, 육, 칠, 팔, 구, 십

Native Korean: 하나, 둘, 셋, 넷, 다섯, 여섯, 일곱, 여덟, 아홉, 열

1 일 [il]
하나 [ha-na]

2 이 [i]
둘 [dul]

3 삼 [sam]
셋 [set]

4 사 [sa]
넷 [net]

5 오 [o]
다섯 [da-seot]

6 육 [yuk]
여섯 [yeo-seot]

7 칠 [chil]
일곱 [il-gop]

8 팔 [pal]
여덟 [yeo-deol]

9 구 [gu]
아홉 [a-hop]

10 십 [sip]
열 [yeol]

모음 Vowels / 자음 Consonants	ㅏ	ㅑ	ㅓ	ㅕ	ㅗ	ㅛ	ㅜ	ㅠ	ㅡ	ㅣ
ㄱ	가	갸	거	겨	고	교	구	규	그	기
ㄴ	나	냐	너	녀	노	뇨	누	뉴	느	니
ㄷ	다	댜	더	뎌	도	됴	두	듀	드	디
ㄹ	라	랴	러	려	로	료	루	류	르	리
ㅁ	마	먀	머	며	모	묘	무	뮤	므	미
ㅂ	바	뱌	버	벼	보	뵤	부	뷰	브	비
ㅅ	사	샤	서	셔	소	쇼	수	슈	스	시
ㅇ	아	야	어	여	오	요	우	유	으	이
ㅈ	자	쟈	저	져	조	죠	주	쥬	즈	지
ㅊ	차	챠	처	쳐	초	쵸	추	츄	츠	치
ㅋ	카	캬	커	켜	코	쿄	쿠	큐	크	키
ㅌ	타	탸	터	텨	토	툐	투	튜	트	티
ㅍ	파	퍄	퍼	펴	포	표	푸	퓨	프	피
ㅎ	하	햐	허	혀	호	효	후	휴	흐	히

타	도	구	미	추	차
기	고	거	기	기	슬

아빠	삼촌	엄마	누나/언니	형/오빠
나	고모	(친)할머니	(외)할머니	
동생	이모	(친)할아버지	(외)할아버지	

부	자	사	라	욱	눈
뉴	나	나	닌	농	

발	손	혀	목
입술	귀	턱	발가락
입	눈	눈썹	코
다리	얼굴	손가락	팔	머리카락

This page is intentionally left blank.

서	부	돈	돌	토	마
도	도	두	독	리	

겨울	봄	여름	가을

콘	비	오	프	우	마
로	리	로	루	리	진

화살표	타원	마름모	별	삼각형/세모
오각형	하트	원/동그라미	사각형/네모	

This page is intentionally left blank.

page 48

자	두	술	소	기	차
마	모	미	미	만	문

page 49

일요일	월요일	수요일
금요일	화요일	토요일
목요일		

page 56

비	지	츠	퀴	채	다
바	부	바	부	반	

page 57

가위	물감	책상	공책
책가방	붓	교과서	연필
풀	색연필	클립	지우개	의자

This page is intentionally left blank.

page 64

박	울	자	랑	건	수
소	수	사	숫	서	

page 65

목도리	모자	장갑	드레스
반바지	자켓	스웨터	양말
티셔츠	치마	잠옷	신발

page 72

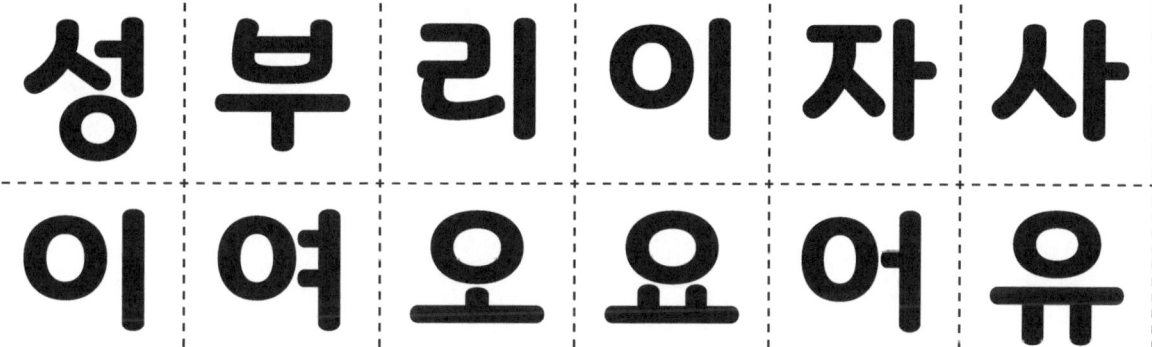

성	부	리	이	자	사
이	여	오	요	어	유

page 73

무서운	화난	슬픈	놀란	부끄러운
흥분된	피곤한	기쁜	떨린	

This page is intentionally left blank.

page 80

울	난	잠	녁	도	두
자	저	지	장	저	감

page 81

목성	금성	수성	해왕성	토성
지구	화성	태양	천왕성	

page 88

솔	충	석	고	구	바
청	출	최	추	칫	지

page 89

야구	수영	배구	테니스	풋볼
골프	농구	스키	축구	

This page is intentionally left blank.

page 96

칼	키	브	트	즈	드
카	퀴	카	큐		

page 97

비행기 　 스쿠터 　 버스 　 자전거 　 자동차

기차 　 오토바이 　 스케이트보드 　 배

page 104

탑	립	자	수	통	코
타	투	툴	탁		

page 105

적다 　 많다 　 크다 　 앞 　 짧다

작다 　 왼쪽 　 뒤 　 오른쪽 　 길다

This page is intentionally left blank.

page 112

노	지	피	니	다	판
페	표	아	피		

page 113

한국	중국	독일	영국
미국	프랑스	호주	인도
캐나다	베트남	브라질	멕시코

page 120

교	허	아	한	하	하
루	글	늘	비	수	학

page 121

신정	부활절	할로윈	크리스마스	아버지의 날
독립기념일	어머니의 날	추수감사절	발렌타인 데이	

This page is intentionally left blank.

Answer Key

page 17

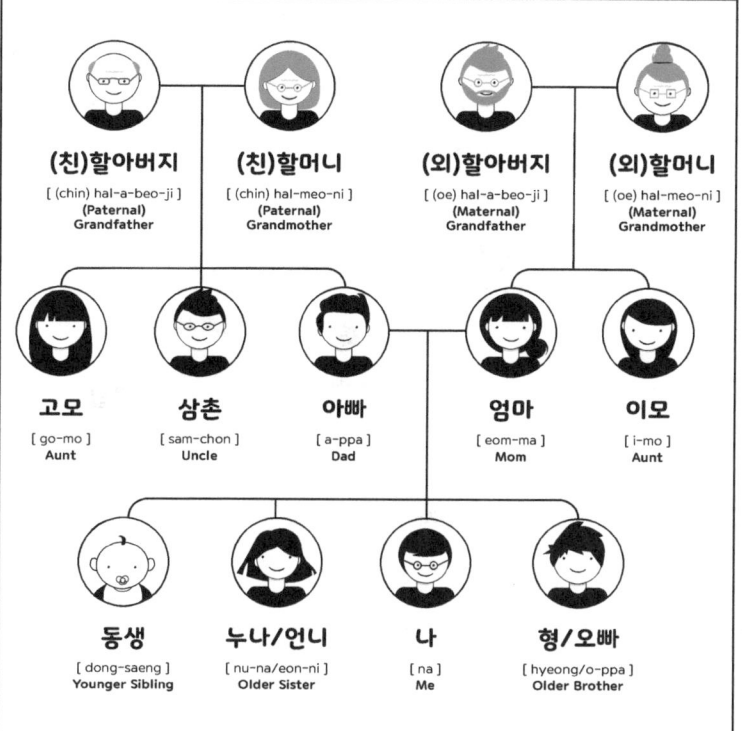

page 25

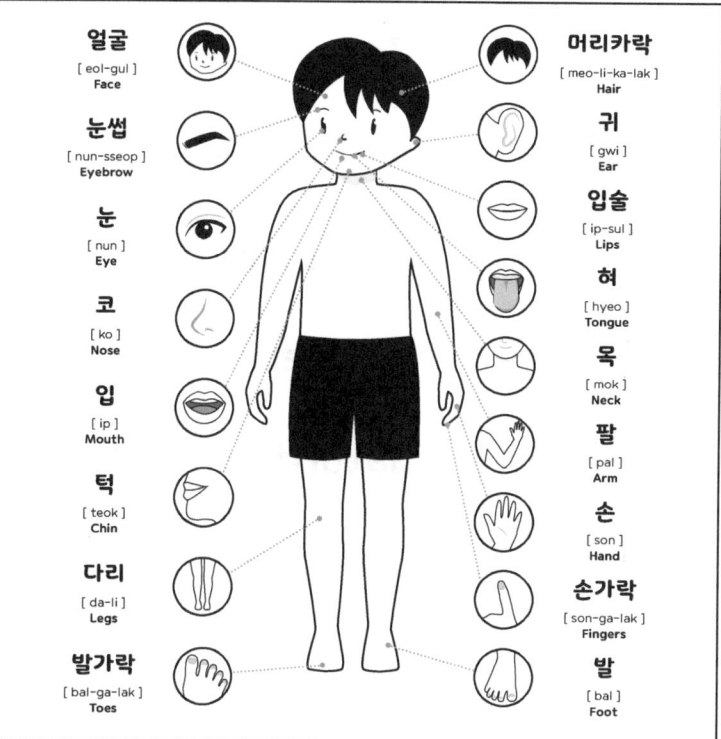

page 33

page 41

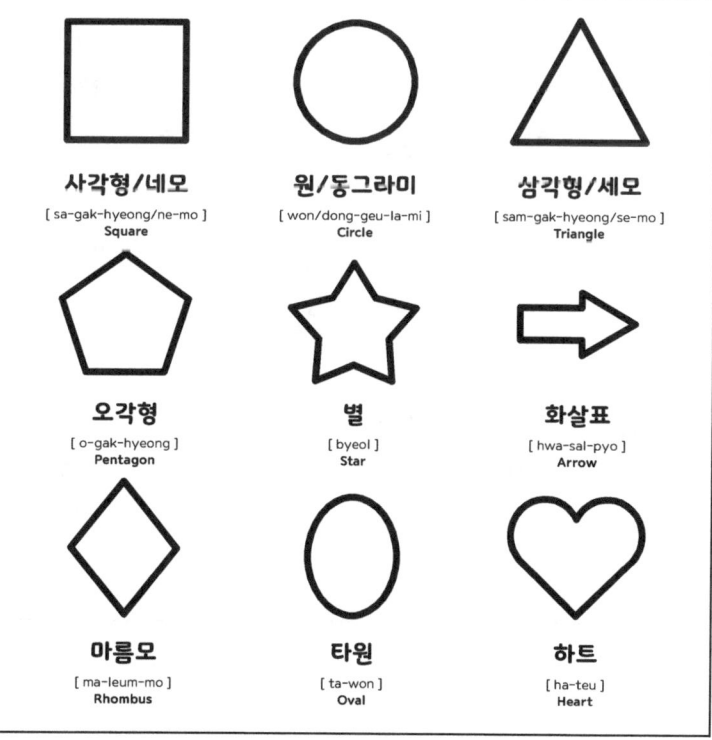

page 49

월요일 [wol-yo-il]	Monday
화요일 [hwa-yo-il]	Tuesday
수요일 [su-yo-il]	Wednesday
목요일 [mok-yo-il]	Thursday
금요일 [geum-yo-il]	Friday
토요일 [to-yo-il]	Saturday
일요일 [il-yo-il]	Sunday

page 57

공책 [gong-chaek] Notebook
가위 [ga-wi] Scissors
색연필 [saek-yeon-pil] Colored Pencil
책가방 [chaek-ga-bang] Schoolbag
연필 [yeon-pil] Pencil
붓 [but] Brush
교과서 [gyo-gwa-seo] Textbook
지우개 [ji-u-gae] Eraser
풀 [pul] Glue
물감 [mul-gam] Paint
클립 [keul-rip] Binder Clip
책상 [chaek-sang] Desk
의자 [eui-ja] Chair

page 65

반바지 [ban-ba-ji] Shorts
목도리 [mok-do-ri] Scarf
스웨터 [seu-we-teo] Sweater
모자 [mo-ja] Hat
양말 [yang-mal] Socks
장갑 [jang-gap] Gloves
자켓 [ja-ket] Jacket
드레스 [deu-re-seu] Dress
치마 [chi-ma] Skirt
티셔츠 [ti-syeo-cheu] T-shirt
신발 [sin-bal] Shoes
잠옷 [jam-ot] Pajamas

page 73

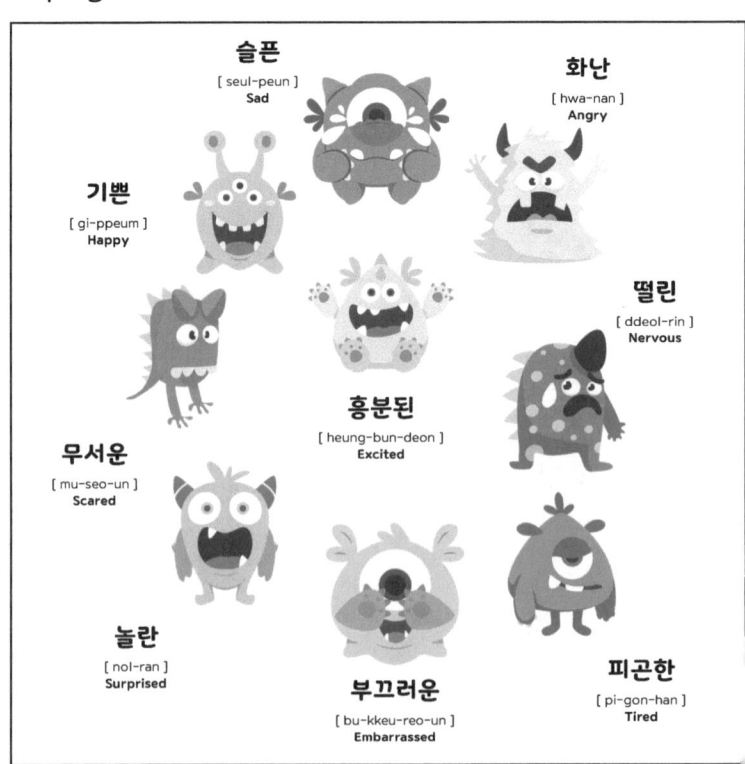

슬픈 [seul-peun] Sad
화난 [hwa-nan] Angry
기쁜 [gi-ppeum] Happy
떨린 [ddeol-rin] Nervous
흥분된 [heung-bun-deon] Excited
무서운 [mu-seo-un] Scared
놀란 [nol-ran] Surprised
부끄러운 [bu-kkeu-reo-un] Embarrassed
피곤한 [pi-gon-han] Tired

page 81

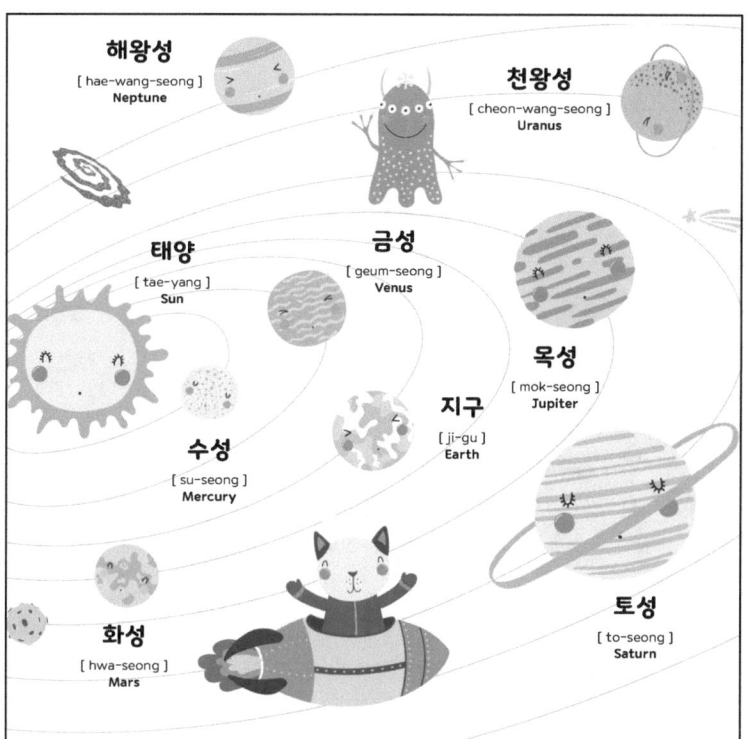

해왕성
[hae-wang-seong]
Neptune

천왕성
[cheon-wang-seong]
Uranus

태양
[tae-yang]
Sun

금성
[geum-seong]
Venus

목성
[mok-seong]
Jupiter

지구
[ji-gu]
Earth

수성
[su-seong]
Mercury

화성
[hwa-seong]
Mars

토성
[to-seong]
Saturn

page 89

야구
[ya-gu]
Baseball

축구
[chuk-gu]
Soccer

농구
[nong-gu]
Basketball

수영
[su-yeong]
Swimming

스키
[seu-ki]
Skiing

골프
[gol-peu]
Golf

배구
[bae-gu]
Volleyball

테니스
[te-ni-seu]
Tennis

풋볼
[put-bol]
Football

page 97

비행기
[bi-haeng-gi]
Airplane

스쿠터
[seu-ku-teo]
Scooter

배
[bae]
Ship/Boat

자동차
[ja-dong-cha]
Car

오토바이
[o-to-ba-i]
Motorcycle

스케이트보드
[seu-ke-i-teu-bo-deu]
Skateboard

버스
[beo-seu]
Bus

자전거
[ja-jeon-geo]
Bicycle

기차
[gi-cha]
Train

page 105

길다
[gil-da]
Tall

짧다
[jjal-da]
Short

크다
[keu-da]
Big

작다
[jak-da]
Small

많다
[man-ta]
More

적다
[jeok-da]
Less

왼쪽
[oen-jjok]
Left

오른쪽
[o-reun-jjok]
Right

앞
[ap]
Front

뒤
[dwi]
Back

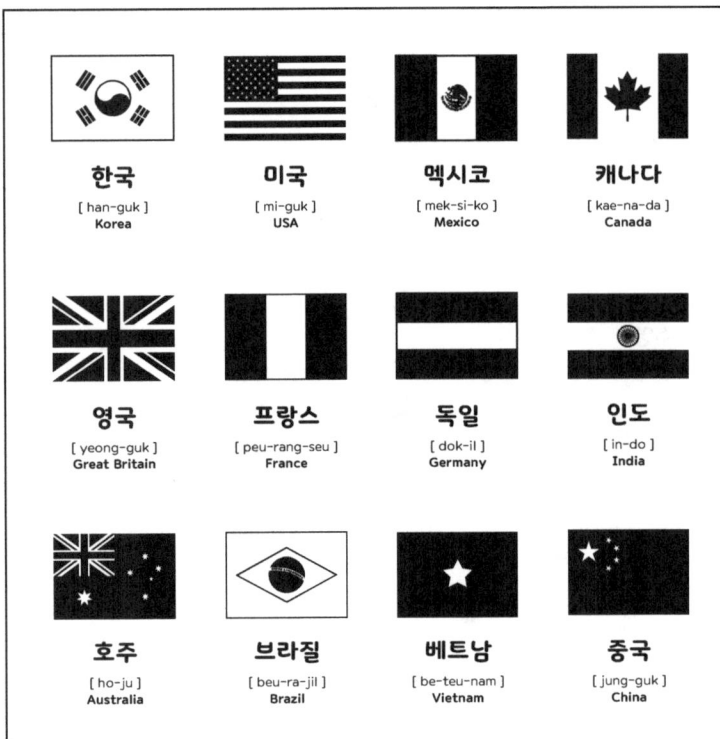

한국
[han-guk]
Korea

미국
[mi-guk]
USA

엑시코
[mek-si-ko]
Mexico

캐나다
[kae-na-da]
Canada

영국
[yeong-guk]
Great Britain

프랑스
[peu-rang-seu]
France

독일
[dok-il]
Germany

인도
[in-do]
India

호주
[ho-ju]
Australia

브라질
[beu-ra-jil]
Brazil

베트남
[be-teu-nam]
Vietnam

중국
[jung-guk]
China

1월
[il-wol]
January

신정
[sin-jeong]
New Year

2월
[i-wol]
February

발렌타인 데이
[bal-ren-ta-in-de-i]
Valentine's Day

3월
[sam-wol]
March

부활절
[bu-hwal-jeol]
Easter

4월
[sa-wol]
April

5월
[o-wol]
May

8월
[pal-wol]
August

독립기념일
[dok-rip-gi-nyeom-il]
Independence Day

7월
[chil-wol]
July

아버지의 날
[a-beo-ji-eu-nal]
Father's Day

6월
[yu-wol]
June

어머니의 날
[eo-meo-ni-eu-nal]
Mother's Day

9월
[gu-wol]
September

할로윈
[hal-ro-win]
Halloween

10월
[si-wol]
October

추수감사절
[chu-su-gam-sa-jeol]
Thanksgiving

11월
[sip-il-wol]
November

크리스마스
[keu-ri-seu-ma-seu]
Christmas

12월
[sip-i-wol]
December

Snap, share, brag!

Follow us on Instagram
#stellarsollearning
@stellarsolcreativelearning

Made in United States
Troutdale, OR
08/27/2024

22354651R00080